Comprehensive Criminal Procedure
Fifth Edition

2022 Supplement

2022 Supplement

Comprehensive Criminal Procedure

Fifth Edition

Ronald Jay Allen

John Henry Wigmore Professor of Law
Northwestern University

Joseph L. Hoffmann

Harry Pratter Professor of Law
Indiana University Maurer School of Law

Debra A. Livingston

United States Circuit Judge, Second Circuit
Paul J. Kellner Professor of Law
Columbia University

Andrew D. Leipold

Edwin M. Adams Professor and Director,
Program in Criminal Law & Procedure
University of Illinois

Tracey L. Meares

Walton Hale Hamilton Professor of Law
Yale Law School

ASPEN PUBLISHING

To contact Customer Service, e-mail customer.service@aspenpublishing.com, call 1-800-950-5259, or mail correspondence to:

Aspen Publishing
Attn: Order Department
PO Box 990
Frederick, MD 21705

Printed in the United States of America.

1 2 3 4 5 6 7 8 9 0

ISBN 978-1-5438-5895-2

About Aspen Publishing

Aspen Publishing is a leading provider of educational content and digital learning solutions to law schools in the U.S. and around the world. Aspen provides best-in-class solutions for legal education through authoritative textbooks, written by renowned authors, and breakthrough products such as Connected eBooks, Connected Quizzing, and PracticePerfect.

The Aspen Casebook Series (famously known among law faculty and students as the "red and black" casebooks) encompasses hundreds of highly regarded textbooks in more than eighty disciplines, from large enrollment courses, such as Torts and Contracts to emerging electives such as Sustainability and the Law of Policing. Study aids such as the *Examples & Explanations* and the *Emanuel Law Outlines* series, both highly popular collections, help law students master complex subject matter.

Major products, programs, and initiatives include:

- **Connected eBooks** are enhanced digital textbooks and study aids that come with a suite of online content and learning tools designed to maximize student success. Designed in collaboration with hundreds of faculty and students, the Connected eBook is a significant leap forward in the legal education learning tools available to students.
- **Connected Quizzing** is an easy-to-use formative assessment tool that tests law students' understanding and provides timely feedback to improve learning outcomes. Delivered through CasebookConnect.com, the learning platform already used by students to access their Aspen casebooks, Connected Quizzing is simple to implement and integrates seamlessly with law school course curricula.
- **PracticePerfect** is a visually engaging, interactive study aid to explain commonly encountered legal doctrines through easy-to-understand animated videos, illustrative examples, and numerous practice questions. Developed by a team of experts, PracticePerfect is the ideal study companion for today's law students.
- The **Aspen Learning Library** enables law schools to provide their students with access to the most popular study aids on the market across all of their courses. Available through an annual subscription, the online library consists of study aids in e-book, audio, and video formats with full text search, note-taking, and highlighting capabilities.
- Aspen's **Digital Bookshelf** is an institutional-level online education bookshelf, consolidating everything students and professors need to ensure success. This program ensures that every student has access to affordable course materials from day one.
- **Leading Edge** is a community centered on thinking differently about legal education and putting those thoughts into actionable strategies. At the core of the program is the Leading Edge Conference, an annual gathering of legal education thought leaders looking to pool ideas and identify promising directions of exploration.

Contents

Table of Cases

Italics indicate principal cases.

PART ONE

THE CRIMINAL PROCESS

Chapter 2

The Idea of Due Process

A. Defining Due Process

Add the following footnote at the end of the second full paragraph on page 66:

FN—One final difficulty: Even if the Due Process Clause is best read as incorporating the Bill of Rights, does it render those rights applicable in state criminal cases in exactly the same manner as they apply to federal criminal cases? (This view is sometimes called "jot for jot" incorporation.) Or do the states have greater flexibility to adjust some of the specific terms of those rights? (This view has been called "dual-track" incorporation.) In Ramos v. Louisiana, 590 U.S. ___ (2020), the Supreme Court overruled Apodaca v. Oregon, 406 U.S. 404 (1972)—a case that, due to a 4-1-4 split, reached the odd result of allowing a state to use non-unanimous juries even though the federal government was prohibited from doing so under the Sixth Amendment—and essentially closed the door, once and for all, on "dual-track" incorporation. See also Timbs v. Indiana, 586 U.S. ___ (2019) (unanimously rejecting Indiana's argument for "dual-track" incorporation of the Excessive Fines Clause of the Eighth Amendment).

PART TWO

THE RIGHT TO COUNSEL—THE LINCHPIN OF CONSTITUTIONAL PROTECTION

Chapter 3

The Right to Counsel and Other Assistance

B. Effective Assistance of Counsel

1. The Meaning of Effective Assistance

Add the following paragraphs just before the final paragraph of the majority opinion in the case of Rompilla v. Beard, on page 176:

. . . Further effort would presumably have unearthed much of the material postconviction counsel found, including testimony from several members of Rompilla's family, whom trial counsel did not interview. Judge Sloviter summarized this evidence:

> "Rompilla's parents were both severe alcoholics who drank constantly. His mother drank during her pregnancy with Rompilla, and he and his brothers eventually developed serious drinking problems. His father, who had a vicious temper, frequently beat Rompilla's mother, leaving her bruised and black-eyed, and bragged about his cheating on her. His parents fought violently, and on at least one occasion his mother stabbed his father. He was abused by his father who beat him when he was young with his hands, fists, leather straps, belts and sticks. All of the children lived in terror. There were no expressions of parental love, affection or approval. Instead, he was subjected to yelling and verbal abuse. His father locked Rompilla and his brother Richard in a small wire mesh dog pen that was filthy and excrement filled. He had an isolated background, and was not allowed to visit other children or to speak to anyone on the phone. They had no indoor plumbing in the house, he slept in the attic with no heat, and the children were not given clothes and attended school in rags." 355 F. 3d, at 279 (citations omitted) (dissenting opinion).

The jury never heard any of this and neither did the mental health experts who examined Rompilla before trial. . . .

Add the following just after the final paragraph of the majority opinion in the case of Rompilla v. Beard, on page 176:

JUSTICE KENNEDY, with whom CHIEF JUSTICE REHNQUIST, JUSTICE SCALIA, and JUSTICE THOMAS join, dissenting:

. . . Under any standard of review the investigation performed by Rompilla's counsel in preparation for sentencing was not only adequate but also conscientious.

. . . Rompilla was represented at trial by Fredrick Charles, the chief public defender for Lehigh County at the time, and Maria Dantos, an assistant public defender. Charles and Dantos were assisted by John Whispell, an investigator in the public defender's office. Rompilla's defense team sought to develop mitigating evidence from various sources. First, they questioned Rompilla extensively about his upbringing and background. To make these conversations more productive they provided Rompilla with a list of the mitigating circumstances recognized by Pennsylvania law. *Id.*, at 657. Cf. *Strickland,* 466 U.S., at 691 ("[W]hen a defendant has given counsel reason to believe that pursuing certain investigations would be fruitless or even harmful, counsel's failure to pursue those investigations may not later be challenged as unreasonable"). Second, Charles and Dantos arranged for Rompilla to be examined by three experienced mental health professionals, experts described by Charles as "the best forensic psychiatrist around here, [another] tremendous psychiatrist and a fabulous forensic psychologist." Finally, Rompilla's attorneys questioned his family extensively in search of any information that might help spare Rompilla the death penalty. Dantos, in particular, developed a "very close" relationship with Rompilla's family, which was a "constant source of information." Indeed, after trial Rompilla's wife sent Dantos a letter expressing her gratitude. The letter referred to Charles and Dantos as "superb human beings" who "fought and felt everything [Rompilla's] family did."

The Court acknowledges the steps taken by Rompilla's attorneys in preparation for sentencing but finds fault nonetheless. "[T]he lawyers were deficient," the Court says, "in failing to examine the court file on Rompilla's prior conviction."

. . . *Strickland* anticipated the temptation "to second-guess counsel's assistance after conviction or adverse sentence" and cautioned that "[a] fair assessment of attorney performance requires that every effort be made to eliminate the distorting effects of hindsight, to reconstruct the circumstances of counsel's challenged conduct, and to evaluate the conduct from counsel's perspective at the time." 466 U.S., at 689. Today, the Court succumbs to the very temptation that *Strickland* warned against. In the process, the majority imposes on defense attorneys a rigid requirement that finds no support in our cases or common sense.

I would affirm the judgment of the Court of Appeals.

Add the following paragraph at the end of Note 7 on page 179:

Two recent *per curiam* opinions may be further evidence that the Court is retreating from a possible broad reading of *Rompilla* to the effect that virtually any possibility of mitigation, including those discovered after the trial, is sufficient to find ineffective assistance of counsel. Shinn v. Kayer, 592 U.S. ___ (2020), involved facts somewhat similar to *Rompilla*, in that the defendant was an unenthusiastic participant in the mitigation effort at trial. On habeas, new counsel identified various avenues of possible mitigation, but the Supreme Court nonetheless found that they were insufficient to grant relief. In Mays v. Hines, 592 U.S. ___ (2021), the allegation was that defense counsel failed to investigate a possible alternative suspect. Although there was perhaps a possibility that someone other than Hines committed the murder, the Court found the probability too low to meet the standard required to grant habeas. It is unclear how much these two cases speak to the actual standard for ineffective assistance, as compared to the standard for federal habeas relief. For relief under habeas, a trial court error must be such that no reasonable jurist could disagree about the proper outcome in light of the Supreme Court's precedents. In other words, it is possible for a trial court to do something that is in fact errone-ous—in the sense that a later Supreme Court decision would determine it to be wrong—but that, at the time, could lead to reasonable disagreement. The last decision of the Court's 2020 Term was yet another *per curiam* opinion indicating the declining influence of *Rompilla.* See Dunn v. Reeves, 592 U.S. ___ (2021).

PART THREE

THE RIGHT TO BE LET ALONE—AN EXAMINATION OF THE FOURTH AND FIFTH AMENDMENTS AND RELATED AREAS

Chapter 5

The Fourth Amendment

A. Remedies

2. Other Remedies

a. Damages

Replace Note 3 on page 332 with the following:

3. This leaves the question of damages liability for police officers. The key doctrine here is qualified immunity—a constitutional fault standard that applies whenever government officials are sued for damages under either §1983 or *Bivens*. In Anderson v. Creighton, 483 U.S. 635 (1987), the Court ruled that damages are available against a police officer who has violated the Fourth Amendment only when he has behaved with something akin to gross negligence—when the governing law and its application to the circumstances facing the officer are clear and he has nonetheless disregarded them. This standard has been interpreted by some courts to require a plaintiff to identify a prior case in which an officer has been held liable for conduct that is essentially identical to the facts presented in her own case—a standard that is practically impossible to meet, motivating Justice Sotomayor to state that the current doctrine "renders the protections of the Fourth Amendment hollow." Mullenix v. Luna, 577 U.S. ___, ___ (2015) (Sotomayor, J., dissenting).

Why limit recovery in this way? After all, a large number of people whose Fourth Amendment rights have been violated will receive no compensation under this regime, thus depriving the damages remedy of one of its chief virtues over exclusion—namely, that it will compensate the *innocent* victim. And, as a policy matter, isn't it difficult to see how police officers will change their behavior if they are rarely if ever required to pay for behavior most people would consider clearly negligent? Professor Joanna Schwartz makes a comprehensive case against the current standard in The Case Against Qualified Immunity, 93 Notre Dame Law Review 1797 (2018).

B. The Scope of the Fourth Amendment

2. The Meaning of "Seizures"

Insert the following Note and main case after Note 4 on page 434:

5. In the following case, the Supreme Court addressed a circuit split arising from the tension between *Brower*'s emphasis on seizure as the "intentional acquisition of physical control" and *Hodari D.*'s distinction between
"seizure by physical force," which can be accomplished by a mere touch,
and by "show of authority plus submission." (This tension is referenced in
Note 3.) The Court declined to repudiate *Hodari D.*'s discussion of seizure
by physical force as mere dicta and instead made clear that the use of
physical force constituting a seizure is not limited to the physical grabbing
of an individual but also includes such force as shooting a suspect as they
are fleeing—even if the suspect manages to escape. This seems perfectly
sensible if one accepts the basic analysis in *Hodari D.* But does the dissent
successfully cast any doubt on whether this analysis makes sense, in the
first instance?

TORRES v. MADRID
Certiorari to the United States Court of Appeals for the Tenth Circuit
592 U.S. ___ (2021)

CHIEF JUSTICE ROBERTS delivered the opinion of the Court.
The Fourth Amendment prohibits unreasonable "seizures" to safeguard
"[t]he right of the people to be secure in their persons." Under our cases,
an officer seizes a person when he uses force to apprehend her. The
question in this case is whether a seizure occurs when an officer shoots
someone who temporarily eludes capture after the shooting. The answer is
yes: The application of physical force to the body of a person with intent
to restrain is a seizure, even if the force does not succeed in subduing the
person.

I

At dawn on July 15, 2014, four New Mexico State Police officers arrived
at an apartment complex in Albuquerque to execute an arrest warrant
for a woman accused of white collar crimes, but also "suspected of having

been involved in drug trafficking, murder, and other violent crimes." App. to Pet. for Cert. 11a. What happened next is hotly contested. We recount the facts in the light most favorable to petitioner Roxanne Torres because the court below granted summary judgment to Officers Janice Madrid and Richard Williamson, the two respondents here.

The officers observed Torres standing with another person near a Toyota FJ Cruiser in the parking lot of the complex. Officer Williamson concluded that neither Torres nor her companion was the target of the warrant. As the officers approached the vehicle, the companion departed, and Torres—at the time experiencing methamphetamine withdrawal—got into the driver's seat. The officers attempted to speak with her, but she did not notice their presence until one of them tried to open the door of her car.

Although the officers wore tactical vests marked with police identification, Torres saw only that they had guns. She thought the officers were carjackers trying to steal her car, and she hit the gas to escape them. Neither Officer Madrid nor Officer Williamson, according to Torres, stood in the path of the vehicle, but both fired their service pistols to stop her. All told, the two officers fired 13 shots at Torres, striking her twice in the back and temporarily paralyzing her left arm.

Steering with her right arm, Torres accelerated through the fusillade of bullets, exited the apartment complex, drove a short distance, and stopped in a parking lot. After asking a bystander to report an attempted carjacking, Torres stole a Kia Soul that happened to be idling nearby and drove 75 miles to Grants, New Mexico. The good news for Torres was that the hospital in Grants was able to airlift her to another hospital where she could receive appropriate care. The bad news was that the hospital was back in Albuquerque, where the police arrested her the next day. She pleaded no contest to aggravated fleeing from a law enforcement officer, assault on a peace officer, and unlawfully taking a motor vehicle.

Torres later sought damages from Officers Madrid and Williamson under 42 U.S.C. § 1983, which provides a cause of action for the deprivation of constitutional rights by persons acting under color of state law. She claimed that the officers applied excessive force, making the shooting an unreasonable seizure under the Fourth Amendment. The District Court granted summary judgment to the officers, and the Court of Appeals for the Tenth Circuit affirmed on the ground that "a suspect's continued flight after being shot by police negates a Fourth Amendment excessive-force claim.". . .

We granted certiorari.

II

. . . This case concerns the "seizure" of a "person," which can take the form of "physical force" or a "show of authority" that "in some way restrain[s] the liberty" of the person. Terry v. Ohio, 392 U.S. 1, 19, n. 16 (1968). The question before us is whether the application of physical force is a seizure if the force, despite hitting its target, fails to stop the person.

We largely covered this ground in California v. Hodari D., 499 U. S. 621 (1991). There we interpreted the term "seizure" by consulting the common law of arrest, the "quintessential 'seizure of the person' under our Fourth Amendment jurisprudence. Id., at 624. As Justice Scalia explained for himself and six other Members of the Court, the common law treated "the mere grasping or application of physical force with lawful authority" as an arrest, "whether or not it succeeded in subduing the arrestee." Ibid.; see id., at 625 ("merely touching" sufficient to constitute an arrest). Put another way, an officer's application of physical force to the body of a person "'for the purpose of arresting him'" was itself an arrest—not an *attempted* arrest—even if the person did not yield. Id., at 624 (quoting Whithead v. Keyes, 85 Mass. 495, 501 (1862)).

The common law distinguished the application of force from a show of authority, such as an order for a suspect to halt. The latter does not become an arrest unless and until the arrestee complies with the demand. As the Court explained in *Hodari D.*, "[a]n arrest requires *either* physical force . . . *or*, where that is absent, *submission* to the assertion of authority." 499 U.S., at 626 (emphasis in original).

Hodari D. articulates two pertinent principles. First, common law arrests are Fourth Amendment seizures. And second, the common law considered the application of force to the body of a person with intent to restrain to be an arrest, no matter whether the arrestee escaped. We need not decide whether *Hodari D.*, which principally concerned a show of authority, controls the outcome of this case as a matter of *stare decisis*, because we independently reach the same conclusions. . . .

At the adoption of the Fourth Amendment, a "seizure" was the "act of taking by warrant" or "of laying hold on suddenly"—for example, when an "officer seizes a thief." 2 N. Webster, An American Dictionary of the English Language 67 (1828) (Webster) (emphasis deleted). A seizure did not necessarily result in actual control or detention. It is true that, when speaking of property, "[f]rom the time of the founding to the present, the word 'seizure' has meant a 'taking possession.'" *Hodari D.*, 499 U.S., at 624 (quoting 2 Webster 67). But the Framers selected a term—seizure—broad enough to apply to all the concerns of the Fourth Amendment: "persons," as well as "houses, papers, and effects." As applied to a person, "[t]he word 'seizure' readily bears the meaning of a laying on of hands or application of physical force to restrain movement, even when it is ultimately unsuccessful." 499 U.S., at 626. Then, as now, an ordinary user of the English language could remark: "She seized the purse-snatcher, but he broke out of her grasp." Ibid. . . .

Because arrests are seizures of a person, *Hodari D.* properly looked to the common law of arrest for "historical understandings 'of what was deemed an unreasonable search and seizure when the Fourth Amendment was adopted.'" Carpenter v. United States, 585 U. S. ___, ___ (2018) (quoting Carroll v. United States, 267 U.S. 132, 149 (1925). . . .

The common law rule identified in *Hodari D.*—that the application of force gives rise to an arrest, even if the officer does not secure control over the arrestee—achieved recognition to such an extent that English lawyers could confidently (and accurately) proclaim that "[a]ll the authorities, from the earliest time to the present, establish that a corporal touch is sufficient to constitute an arrest, even though the defendant do not submit." Nicholl v. Darley, 2 Y. & J. 399, 400, 148 Eng. Rep. 974 (Exch. 1828) (citing Hodges v. Marks, Cro. Jac. 485, 79 Eng. Rep. 414 (K. B. 1615)). The slightest application of force could satisfy this rule. In Genner v. Sparks, 6 Mod. 173, 87 Eng. Rep. 928 (Q. B. 1704), the defendant did not submit to the authority of an arrest warrant, but the court explained that the bailiff would have made an arrest if he "had but touched the defendant even with the end of his finger." Ibid., 87 Eng. Rep., at 929. So too, if a "bailiff caught one by the hand (whom he had a warrant to arrest) as he held it out of a window," that alone would accomplish an arrest. Anonymus, 1 Vent. 306, 86 Eng. Rep. 197 (K. B. 1677). . . .

Early American courts adopted this mere-touch rule from England, just as they embraced other common law principles of search and seizure. See Wilson v. Arkansas, 514 U.S. 927, 933 (1995). . . .

This case, of course, does not involve "laying hands," Sheriff v. Godfrey, 7 Mod. 288, 289, 87 Eng. Rep. 1247 (K. B. 1739), but instead a shooting. Neither the parties nor the United States as *amicus curiae* suggests that the officers' use of bullets to restrain Torres alters the analysis in any way. And we are aware of no common law authority addressing an arrest under such circumstances, or indeed any case involving an application of force from a distance. . . .

[W]e see no basis for drawing an artificial line between grasping with a hand and other means of applying physical force to effect an arrest. The dissent . . . argues that the common law limited arrests by force to the literal placement of hands on the suspect, because no court published an opinion discussing a suspect who continued to flee after being hit with a bullet or some other weapon. See *post* (opinion of Gorsuch, J.). This objection calls to mind the unavailing defense of the person who "persistently denied that he had laid hands upon a priest, for he had only cudgelled and kicked him." 2 S. Pufendorf, De Jure Naturae et Gentium 795 (C. Oldfather & W. Oldfather transl. 1934). The required "corporal seising or touching the defendant's body" can be as readily accomplished by a bullet as by the end of a finger. 3 Blackstone 288.

We will not carve out this greater intrusion on personal security from the mere-touch rule just because founding-era courts did not confront apprehension by firearm. While firearms have existed for a millennium and were certainly familiar at the founding, we have observed that law enforcement did not carry handguns until the latter half of the 19th century, at which point "it bec[a]me possible to use deadly force from a distance as a means of apprehension." Tennessee v. Garner, 471 U.S. 1, 14–15 (1985). So it should come as no surprise that neither we nor the dissent has located a common law case in which an officer used a gun to apprehend a suspect. But the focus of the Fourth Amendment is "the privacy and security of individuals," not the particular manner of "arbitrary invasion[ ] by governmental officials." Camara v. Municipal Court of City and County of San Francisco, 387 U.S. 523, 528 (1967). As noted, our precedent protects "that degree of privacy against government that existed when the Fourth Amendment was adopted," Kyllo v. United States, 533 U.S. 27, 34 (2001)—a protection that extends to "[s]ubtler and more far-reaching means of invading privacy" adopted only later, Olmstead v. United States, 277 U.S. 438, 473 (1928) (Brandeis, J., dissenting). There is nothing subtle about a bullet, but the Fourth Amendment preserves personal security with respect to methods of apprehension old and new.

We stress, however, that the application of the common law rule does not transform every physical contact between a government employee and a member of the public into a Fourth Amendment seizure. A seizure requires the use of force *with intent to restrain*. Accidental force will not qualify. See County of Sacramento v. Lewis, 523 U.S. 833, 844 (1998). Nor will force intentionally applied for some other purpose satisfy this rule. In this opinion, we consider only force used to apprehend. We do not accept the dissent's invitation to opine on matters not presented here—pepper spray, flash-bang grenades, lasers, and more.

Moreover, the appropriate inquiry is whether the challenged conduct *objectively* manifests an intent to restrain, for we rarely probe the subjective motivations of police officers in the Fourth Amendment context. . . . While a mere touch can be enough for a seizure, the amount of force remains pertinent in assessing the objective intent to restrain. A tap on the shoulder to get one's attention will rarely exhibit such an intent.

Nor does the seizure depend on the subjective perceptions of the seized person. Here, for example, Torres claims to have perceived the officers' actions as an attempted carjacking. But the conduct of the officers—ordering Torres to stop and then shooting to restrain her movement—satisfies the objective test for a seizure, regardless whether Torres comprehended the governmental character of their actions.

The rule we announce today is narrow. In addition to the requirement of intent to restrain, a seizure by force—absent submission—lasts only as long as the application of force. That is to say that the Fourth Amendment does not recognize any "*continuing* arrest during the period of fugitivity." *Hodari D.*, 499 U. S., at 625. The fleeting nature of some seizures by force undoubtedly may inform what damages a civil plaintiff may recover, and what evidence a criminal defendant may exclude from trial. But brief seizures are seizures all the same.

Applying these principles to the facts viewed in the light most favorable to Torres, the officers' shooting applied physical force to her body and objectively manifested an intent to restrain her from driving away. We therefore conclude that the officers seized Torres for the instant that the bullets struck her.

III

. . . The officers and their *amici* stress that common law rules are not automatically "elevated to constitutional proscriptions," *Hodari D.*, 499 U.S., at 626, n. 2, especially if they are "distorted almost beyond recognition when literally applied," *Garner*, 471 U.S., at 15. In their view, the common law doctrine recognized in *Hodari D.* is just "a narrow legal rule intended to govern liability in civil cases involving debtors." Brief for National Association of Counties et al. as *Amici Curiae* 12. The dissent presses the same argument.

But the common law did not define the arrest of a debtor any differently from the arrest of a felon. Whether the arrest was authorized by a criminal indictment or a civil writ, "there must be a corporal seizing, or touching the defendant's person; or, what is tantamount, a power of taking immediate possession of the body, and the party's submission thereto, and a declaration of the officer that he makes an arrest." 1 J. Backus, A Digest of Laws Relating to the Offices and Duties of Sheriff, Coroner and Constable 115–116 (1812). Treatises on the law governing criminal arrests cited Genner v. Sparks, 6 Mod. 173, 87 Eng. Rep. 928—the preeminent mere-touch case involving a debtor—for the proposition that, "[i]n making the arrest, the constable or party making it should actually seize or touch the offender's body, or otherwise restrain his liberty." 1 R. Burn, The Justice of the Peace 275 (28th ed. 1837). . . . American courts likewise articulated a materially identical definition in criminal cases—that "[t]he arrest itself is the laying hands on the defendant," State v. Townsend, 5 Del. 487, 488 (Ct. Gen. Sess. 1854), or that an arrest is "the taking, seizing, or detaining of the person of another, either by touching him or putting hands on him," McAdams v. State, 30 Okla.Crim. 207, 210, 235 P. 241, 242 (1925).

. . . To be sure, the mere-touch rule was particularly well documented in cases involving the execution of civil process. An officer pursuing a debtor could not forcibly enter the debtor's home unless the debtor had escaped arrest, such as by fleeing after being touched. See Semayne's Case, 5 Co. Rep. 91a, 91b, 77 Eng. Rep. 194, 196 (K. B. 1604). Officers seeking to execute criminal process, on the other hand, possessed greater pre-arrest authority to enter a felon's home. See *Payton*, 445 U.S., at 598. But the fact that the common law rules of arrest generated more litigation in the civil context proves only that creditors had ready recourse to the courts to pursue escape actions for unsatisfactory arrests. There is no reason to suspect that English jurists silently adopted a special definition of arrest only for debt collection—indeed, they told us just the opposite. . . .

The officers and the dissent derive from our cases a different touchstone for the seizure of a person: "an intentional acquisition of physical control." Brower v. County of Inyo, 489 U.S. 593, 596 (1989). Under their alternative rule, the use of force becomes a seizure "only when there is a governmental termination of freedom of movement through means intentionally applied." Id., at 597 (emphasis deleted).

This approach improperly erases the distinction between seizures by *control* and seizures by *force*. In all fairness, we too have not always been attentive to this distinction when a case did not implicate the issue. . . .

Unlike a seizure by force, a seizure by acquisition of control involves either voluntary submission to a show of authority or the termination of freedom of movement. A prime example of the latter comes from *Brower*, where the police seized a driver when he crashed into their roadblock.

489 U.S., at 598–599; see also, e.g., Scott v. Harris, 550 U.S. 372, 385 (2007) (ramming car off road); Williams v. Jones, Cas. t. Hard. 299, 301, 95 Eng. Rep. 193, 194 (K. B. 1736) (locking person in room). Under the common law rules of arrest, actual control is a necessary element for this type of seizure. See Wilgus, Arrest Without a Warrant, 22 Mich. L. Rev. 541, 553 (1924). . . .

As common law courts recognized, any such requirement of control would be difficult to apply in cases involving the application of force. At the most basic level, it will often be unclear when an officer succeeds in gaining control over a struggling suspect. Courts will puzzle over whether an officer exercises control when he grabs a suspect, when he tackles him, or only when he slaps on the cuffs. Neither the officers nor the dissent explains how long the control must be maintained—only for a moment, into the squad car, or all the way to the station house. To cite another example, counsel for the officers speculated that the shooting would have been a seizure if Torres stopped "maybe 50 feet" or "half a block" from the scene of the shooting to allow the officers to promptly acquire control. Tr. of Oral Arg. 45. . . .

IV

The dissent sees things differently. It insists that the term "seizure" has always entailed a taking of possession, whether the officer is seizing a person, a ship, or a promissory note. But the facts of the cases and the language of the opinions confirm that the concept of possession included the "constructive detention" of persons "never actually brought within the physical control of the party making an arrest." Wilgus, 22 Mich. L. Rev., at 556 (emphasis deleted); see, e.g., Nicholl, 2 Y. & J., at 404, 148 Eng. Rep., at 976 (explaining that the "slightest touch" can constitute "custody"); Anonymus, 1 Vent., at 306, 86 Eng. Rep., at 197 (describing a touch as a "taking" of a person). . . .

. . . The dissent argues that we advance a "schizophrenic reading of the word 'seizure.'" But our cases demonstrate the unremarkable proposition that the nature of a seizure can depend on the nature of the object being seized. It is not surprising that the concept of constructive detention or the mere-touch rule developed in the context of seizures of a person—capable of fleeing and with an interest in doing so—rather than seizures of "houses, papers, and effects."

The dissent also criticizes us for "posit[ing] penumbras" of "privacy" and "personal security" in our analysis of the Fourth Amendment. But the *text* of the Fourth Amendment expressly guarantees the "right of the people to be *secure* in their *persons*," and our earliest precedents recognized privacy as the "essence" of the Amendment—not some penumbral emanation. Boyd [v. United States], 116 U.S. [616,] 630. . . .

The dissent speculates that the real reason for today's decision is an "impulse" to provide relief to Torres, or maybe a desire "to make life easier for ourselves." It may even be, says the dissent, that the Court "at least hopes to be seen as trying" to achieve particular goals. There is no call for such surmise. At the end of the day we simply agree with the analysis of the common law of arrest and its relation to the Fourth Amendment set forth thirty years ago by Justice Scalia, joined by six of his colleagues, rather than the competing view urged by the dissent today.

* * *

We hold that the application of physical force to the body of a person with intent to restrain is a seizure even if the person does not submit and is not subdued. Of course, a seizure is just the first step in the analysis. The Fourth Amendment does not forbid all or even most seizures—only unreasonable ones. All we decide today is that the officers seized Torres by shooting her with intent to restrain her movement. We leave open on remand any questions regarding the reasonableness of the seizure, the damages caused by the seizure, and the officers' entitlement to qualified immunity. . . .

JUSTICE BARRETT took no part in the consideration or decision of this case.

JUSTICE GORSUCH, with whom JUSTICE THOMAS and JUSTICE ALITO join, dissenting.

The majority holds that a criminal suspect can be simultaneously seized and roaming at large. On the majority's account, a Fourth Amendment "seizure" takes place whenever an officer "merely touches" a suspect. It's a seizure even if the suspect refuses to stop, evades capture, and rides off into the sunset never to be seen again. That view is as mistaken as it is novel.

Until today, a Fourth Amendment "seizure" has required taking possession of someone or something. To reach its contrary judgment, the majority must conflate a seizure with its attempt and confuse an arrest with a battery. In the process, too, the majority must disregard the Constitution's original and ordinary meaning, dispense with our conventional interpretive rules, and bypass the main currents of the common law. Unable to rely on any of these traditional sources of authority, the majority is left to lean on (really, repurpose) an abusive and long-abandoned English debt-collection practice. But there is a reason why, in two centuries filled with litigation over the Fourth Amendment's meaning, this Court has never before adopted the majority's definition of a "seizure." Neither the Constitution nor common sense can sustain it.

I

This case began when two Albuquerque police officers approached Roxanne Torres on foot. The officers thought Ms. Torres was the subject of an arrest warrant and suspected of involvement in murder and drug trafficking. As it turned out, they had the wrong person; Ms. Torres was the subject of a *different* arrest warrant. As she saw the officers walk toward her, Ms. Torres responded by getting into her car and hitting the gas. . . . Fearing the oncoming car was about to hit them, the officers fired their duty weapons, and two bullets struck Ms. Torres while others hit her car.

None of that stopped Ms. Torres. She continued driving—over a curb, across some landscaping, and into a street, eventually colliding with another vehicle. Abandoning her car, she promptly stole a different one parked nearby. Ms. Torres then drove over 75 miles to another city. When she eventually sought medical treatment, doctors decided she needed to be airlifted back to Albuquerque for more intensive care. Only at that point, a day after her encounter with the officers, was Ms. Torres finally identified and arrested. . . .

More than two years later, Ms. Torres sued the officers for damages in federal court under 42 U.S.C. § 1983. She alleged that they had violated the Fourth Amendment by unreasonably "seizing" her. After discovery, the officers moved for summary judgment. The district court granted the motion, and the court of appeals affirmed. Individuals like Ms. Torres are free to sue officers under New Mexico state law for assault or battery. They may also sue officers under the Fourteenth Amendment for conduct that "shocks the conscience." But under longstanding circuit precedent, the courts explained, a Fourth Amendment "seizure" occurs only when the government obtains "physical control" over a person or object. Because Ms. Torres "managed to elude the police for at least a full day after being shot," the courts reasoned, the officers' bullets had not "seized" her; any seizure took place only when she was finally arrested back in Albuquerque the following day.

Now before us, Ms. Torres argues that this Court's decision in California v. Hodari D., 499 U.S. 621(1991), "compel[s] reversal." As she reads it, *Hodari D.* held that a Fourth Amendment seizure takes place

whenever an officer shoots or even "mere[ly] touch[es]" an individual
with the intent to restrain.

Whatever one thinks of Ms. Torres's argument, one thing is certain:
Hodari D. has generated considerable confusion. There, officers chased
a suspect on foot. Later, the suspect argued that he was "seized" for purposes of the Fourth Amendment the moment the chase began. Though
he fled, the suspect argued, a "reasonable person" would not have felt at
liberty given the officers' "show of authority," so a Fourth Amendment
seizure had occurred.

The Court rejected this argument. In doing so, it explained that,
"[f]rom the time of the founding to the present, the word 'seizure' has
meant a 'taking possession.'" Id., at 624. Because the defendant did not
submit to the officers' show of authority, the Court reasoned, the officers'
conduct amounted at most to an attempted seizure. See id., at 626, and
n. 2. And "neither usage nor common-law tradition makes an *attempted*
seizure a seizure." Ibid.

At the same time, . . . the Court didn't end its discussion there. It pro-
ceeded to imagine a different and hypothetical case, one in which the
officers not only chased the suspect but also "appl[ied] physical force"
to him. In these circumstances, the Court suggested, "merely touching"
a suspect, even when officers fail to gain possession, might qualify as a
seizure. Id., at 624–625.

Unsurprisingly, these dueling passages in *Hodari D.* led to a circuit split.
For the first time, some lower courts began holding that a "mere touch"
constitutes a Fourth Amendment "seizure." Others, however, continued to
adhere to the view, taken "[f]rom the time of the founding to the present,"
that the word "seizure" means "taking possession." Id., at 624. We took
this case to sort out the confusion.

II

As an initial matter, Ms. Torres is mistaken that *Hodari D.*'s discussion of
"mere touch" seizures compels a ruling in her favor. Under the doctrine
of *stare decisis*, we normally afford prior holdings of this Court considerable
respect. But, in the course of issuing their holdings, judges sometimes
include a "witty opening paragraph, the background information on how
the law developed," or "digressions speculating on how similar hypothetical
cases might be resolved." B. Garner et al., The Law of Judicial Precedent
44 (2016). Such asides are dicta. The label is hardly an epithet: "Dicta
may afford litigants the benefit of a fuller understanding of the court's
decisional path or related areas of concern." Id., at 65. Dicta can also "be

a source of advice to successors." Ibid. But whatever utility it may have, dicta cannot bind future courts. . . .

On any account, the passage in *Hodari D.* Ms. Torres seeks to invoke was dicta. The only question presented in that case was whether officers seize a defendant by a show of authority *without* touching him. The Court answered that question in the negative. The separate question whether a "mere touch" *also* qualifies as a seizure was not presented by facts of the case. No party briefed the issue. And the opinion offered the matter only shallow consideration, resting on just three sources: A state court opinion from the 1860s, a "comment" in the 1934 Restatement of Torts, and a 1930s legal treatise.

III

[T]he majority picks up where *Hodari D.*'s dicta left off. It contends that an officer "seizes" a person by merely touching him with an "intent to restrain." We are told that a touch is a seizure even if the suspect never stops or slows down; it's a seizure even if he evades capture. In all the years before *Hodari D.*'s dicta, this conclusion would have sounded more than a little improbable to most lawyers and judges—as it should still today. A mere touch may be a battery. It may even be part of an attempted seizure. But the Fourth Amendment's text, its history, and our precedent all confirm that "seizing" something doesn't mean touching it; it means taking possession.

Start with the text. The Fourth Amendment guarantees that "[t]he right of the people to be secure in their persons, houses, papers, and effects, against unreasonable searches and seizures, shall not be violated." As at least part of *Hodari D.* recognized, "[f]rom the time of the founding to the present," the key term here—"seizure"—has always meant " 'taking possession.'" 499 U.S., at 624.

Countless contemporary dictionaries define a "seizure" or the act of "seizing" in terms of possession. This Court's early cases reflect the same understanding. Just sixteen years after the Fourth Amendment's adoption, Congress passed a statute regulating the "seizure" of ships. See The Josefa Segunda, 10 Wheat. 312, 322, 6 L.Ed. 320 (1825). This Court interpreted the term to require "an open, visible possession claimed," so that those previously possessing the ship "understand that they are dispossessed, and that they are no longer at liberty to exercise any dominion on board of the ship." Id., at 325. . . .

Today's majority disputes none of this. It accepts that a seizure of the inanimate objects mentioned in the Fourth Amendment (houses, papers, and effects) requires possession. And when it comes to persons, the majority agrees (as *Hodari D.* held) that a seizure in response to a "show of authority" takes place if and when the suspect submits to an officer's possession. The majority insists that a different rule should apply *only* in cases where an officer "touches" the suspect. Here—and here alone—possession is not required. So, under the majority's logic, we are quite literally asked to believe the officers in this case "seized" Ms. Torres's person, but *not* her car, when they shot both and both continued speeding down the highway.

The majority's need to resort to such a schizophrenic reading of the word "seizure" should be a signal that something has gone seriously wrong. The Fourth Amendment's Search and Seizure Clause uses the word "seizures" once in connection with four objects (persons, houses, papers, and effects). The text thus suggests parity, not disparity, in meaning. . . .The majority's conclusion that a single use of the word "seizures" bears two different meanings at the same time—indeed, in this very case—is truly novel. And when it comes to construing the Constitution, that kind of innovation is no virtue.

If more textual evidence were needed, the Fourth Amendment's neighboring Warrant Clause would seem to provide it. That Clause states that warrants must describe "the persons or things to be seized." Once more, the Amendment uses the same verb—"seized"—for both persons and objects. Once more, it suggests parity, not some hidden divergence between people and their possessions. Nor does anyone dispute that a warrant for the "seizure" of a person means a warrant authorizing officers to take that person into their *possession.*

Against all these adverse textual clues, the majority offers little in reply. . . .

Instead, the majority proceeds to reason that the word "seizure" *must* carry a different meaning for persons and objects because persons alone are "capable of fleeing" and have "an interest in doing so." Ibid. But that reasoning faces trouble even from *Hodari D.,* which explained that "[a] ship still fleeing, even though under attack, would not be considered to have been seized as a war prize." 499 U.S., at 624. Of course, as the majority observes, persons alone can possess "an interest" in fleeing. But, as *Hodari D.*'s example shows, they can have as much (or more) interest in fleeing to prevent the seizure of their possessions as they do their persons. Even today, a suspect driving a car loaded with illegal drugs may be more interested in fleeing to avoid the loss of her valuable cargo than to prevent her own detention. Yet the majority offers no reasoned explanation why the meaning of the word "seizure" changes when officers hit the suspect and when they hit her drugs and car as all three speed away.

Unable to muster any precedent or sound reason for its reading, the majority opinion finishes its textual analysis with a selective snippet from Webster's Dictionary and a hypothetical about a purse snatching. The majority notes that Webster equated a seizure with "'the act of taking by warrant'" or "'laying hold on suddenly.'" But Webster used the warrant definition to describe "the seizure of contraband goods"—a seizure the majority *agrees* requires possession. Meanwhile, the phrase "laying hold on" a person connotes physical possession, as a look at the dictionary's entire definition demonstrates. A "seizure," Webster continued, is the "act of taking possession by force," the "act of taking by warrant," "possession," and "a catching." Read in full, Webster thus lends no support to the majority's view.

The purse hypothetical, borrowed from *Hodari D.*'s dicta, turns out to be even less illuminating. It supposes that "an ordinary user of the English language could remark: 'She seized the purse-snatcher, but he broke out of her grasp'" (quoting *Hodari D.*, 499 U. S., at 626). But what does that prove? The hypothetical contemplates a woman who *takes possession* of the purse-snatcher, establishing a "grasp" for him to "break out of." One doesn't "break out of " a mere touch.

Really, the majority's answer to the Constitution's text is to ignore it. The majority stands mute before the consensus among founding-era dictionaries, this Court's early cases interpreting the word "seizure," and the Warrant Clause. It admits its interpretation spurns the canonical interpretive principle that a single word in a legal text does not change its meaning depending on what object it modifies. All we're offered is a curated snippet and an unhelpful hypothetical. Ultimately, it's hard not to wonder whether the majority says so little about the Constitution's terms because so little can be said that might support its ruling.

Rather than focus on text, the majority turns quickly to history. At common law, it insists, a "linkage" existed between the "seizure" of a person and the concept of an "arrest." Thus, the majority contends, we must examine how the common law defined *that* term. But following the majority down this path only leads to another dead end. Unsurprisingly, an "arrest" at common law ordinarily required possession too.

Consider what some of our usual common law guides say on the subject. Blackstone defined "an arrest" in the criminal context as "the apprehending or restraining of one's person, in order to be forthcoming to answer an alleged or suspected crime." 4 Commentaries on the Laws of England 286 (1769). Hale and Hawkins both equated an "arrest" with "apprehending," "taking," and "detain[ing]" a person. See 1 M. Hale, Pleas of the Crown 89, 93–94 (5th ed. 1716); 2 W. Hawkins, Pleas of the Crown 74–75, 77,

80–81, 86 (3d ed. 1739). And Hawkins stated that an arrest required the officer to "actually have" the suspect "in his Custody." Id., at 129. . . .

Common law causes of action point to the same common-sense conclusion. During the founding era, an individual who was unlawfully arrested could seek redress through the tort of false imprisonment. See 3 W. Blackstone, Commentaries on the Laws of England 127 (1768). That cause of action aimed to remedy "the violation of the right of personal liberty," 3 Blackstone, *supra*, at 127, which was "the power of loco-motion, of changing situation, or removing one's person to whatsoever place one's own inclination may direct," 1 W. Blackstone, Commentaries on the Laws of England 130 (1765). Thus, false imprisonment—the violation of the right to move where one desired—required proof of "[t]he detention of the person" and "[t]he unlawfulness of such detention." 3 Blackstone, *supra*, at 127. That detention could occur "in a gaol, house, stocks, or in the street," but it occurred only if a person was "*under the custody* of another." 1 E. East, Pleas of the Crown 428 (1806) (emphasis added). . . .

Unable to identify anything helpful in the main current of the common law, the majority is forced to retreat to an obscure eddy. Starting from *Hodari D.*'s three references to "mere touch" arrests, the majority traces these authorities back to their English origins. The tale that unfolds is a curious one.

Before bankruptcy reforms in the 19th century, creditors seeking to induce repayment of their loans could employ bailiffs to civilly arrest delinquent debtors and haul them off to debtors prison. But the common law also offered debtors some tools to avoid or delay that fate. Relevant here, the common law treated the home as a "castle of defence and asylum" so no bailiff could break into a debtor's home to effect a civil arrest. 3 Blackstone, *supra*, at 288. Over time, the practice of "keeping house" became an increasingly popular way for debtors to evade the bailiff. Id., at 234. Naturally, too, creditors railed against this "notorious" practice. See ibid. And eventually Parliament responded to their clamor. The English bankruptcy statutes of 1542 and 1570 imposed serious penalties on debtors who "kept house" to avoid imprisonment.

It was seemingly against this backdrop that the strange cases *Hodari D.*'s dicta briefly alluded to and the majority has now dug up began to appear. Under their terms, a bailiff who could manage to touch a person hiding in his home, often through an open window or door, was deemed to have effected a civil "arrest." See Genner v. Sparks, 6 Mod. 173, 87 Eng. Rep. 928 (K. B. 1704). And because this mere touch was deemed an "arrest," the bailiff was then permitted by law to proceed to "br[eak] the house . . .

to seize upon" the person and render him to prison. Ibid., 87 Eng. Rep., at 929. Of course it was farcical to call a tap through an open window an "arrest." But it proved a useful farce, at least for creditors. . . .

By everyone's account, however, the farce extended only so far. Yes, the mere-touch arrest was a feature of civil bankruptcy practice for an unfortunate period. But the majority has not identified a *single* founding-era case extending the mere-touch arrest rule to the criminal context. . . .

So what relevance do these obscure and long-abandoned civil debt-collection practices have for today's case concerning a criminal arrest and brought under the Fourth Amendment? The answer seems to be not much, for at least three reasons.

In the first place, the Amendment speaks of "seizures," not "arrests." To the extent the common law of arrests informs the Amendment's meaning, we have already seen that an arrest normally meant taking possession of an arrestee. Maybe in one peculiar area, and for less than admirable reasons, the common law deviated from this understanding. But this Court usually presumes that those who wrote the Constitution used words in their ordinary sense, not in some idiosyncratic way. . . .

Second, even if we were to hypothesize that people *did* understand the Fourth Amendment to incorporate this quirky rule, what would that tell us? Here, the officers tried to arrest Ms. Torres in a parking lot on behalf of the State for serious crimes, not break into her home on behalf of the local credit union for missing a payment. So even if we were willing to suppose that the founding generation understood the Constitution to incorporate the majority's civil debt-collection arrest rule, nothing before us suggests they contemplated, let alone endorsed, injecting it into the criminal law and overriding settled doctrine equating arrests with possession.

Finally, even in the civil debt-collection context, the majority cannot point to even a single case suggesting that hitting a suspect with an object— an arrow, a bullet, a cudgel, *anything*—as she flees amounted to an arrest. Instead, the majority's cases hold only that the "laying of hands" on an arrestee constituted an arrest. Thus, even if the Fourth Amendment did transpose the "mere touch" rule from the context of civil arrests into the criminal arena, it *still* would not reach this case.

How does the majority respond? Again, it does little more than disregard the difficulties. The majority says there is "no reason to suspect" the common law defined criminal arrests of felons "any differently" than civil arrests of debtors. But the majority skips over all the evidence canvassed above showing that a criminal arrest required possession, not a mere touch. It sails past its failure to identify *any* case holding that a mere touch qualified as a criminal arrest. It ignores the fact Blackstone defined criminal and civil arrests differently.[4] And it claims to find support in Hawkins's statement that an officer could break into a house to capture an arrestee who escaped after being "'lawfully arrested for *any* Cause'" (quoting 2 Pleas of the Crown 87 (1721)). Yet, the question before us isn't what an officer might do *after* making an arrest; it's what constitutes an arrest *in the first place.*

Rather than confront shortcomings like these, the majority asks us to glide past them. It suggests that importing the mere-touch rule into the criminal context is permissible because "no common law case" had occasion to reject that idea expressly. But this gets things backwards. Today, for the first time, the majority seeks to equate seizures and criminal arrests with mere touches, attempted seizures, and batteries. It is for *the majority* to show the Fourth Amendment commands this result. No amount of rhetorical maneuvering can obscure how flat it has fallen . . . .

The majority asks us to glide past another problem too. It acknowledges that its debt-collection cases required a "laying on of hands" to complete an arrest. But it says we should overlook that rule as an accident of antiquity. "Touchings" by "firearm," we are told, were unknown to "founding-era courts," and no "officer used a gun to apprehend a suspect" before 1850. Never mind the shot heard round the world in 1775 and the adoption of the Second Amendment. Never mind that as early as 1592, when a bailiff "feared resistance" and thus "brought with him" a gun "to arrest" someone, a common law court deemed it lawful because "[t]he sheriff or any of his ministers may for the better execution of justice carry with them offensive or defensive weapons." Seint John's Case, 5 Co. Rep. 71b, 77 Eng. Rep. 162, 162–163 (K. B. 1592). Never mind that even tax collectors were carrying guns by the 1680s. E.g., Dickenson v. Watson, Jones, T. 205, 205–206, 84 Eng. Rep. 1218, 1218–1219 (K. B. 1682). And never mind, too, that the majority's problem isn't limited to guns. It fails to cite any case in which a touching by *any* weapon was deemed sufficient to effect an arrest. Seemingly, the majority would have us believe that bailiffs wielding anything but their fists were beyond the framers' imagination. . . .

---

4. The majority cites only Blackstone's definition of a civil arrest, which required a "corporal seising or touching the defendant's body" (quoting 3 W. Blackstone, Commentaries on the Laws of England 288 (1768)). But flipping from Blackstone's third volume (discussing "private wrongs") to his fourth volume (discussing "public wrongs") reveals—as we have already seen but the majority fails to acknowledge—that Blackstone equated a criminal arrest with "apprehending or restraining . . . one's person, in order to be forthcoming to answer an alleged or suspected crime."

[T]he majority . . . asks us to dispense with the common law's "laying on of hands" requirement as an "artificial" rule. Distinguishing between "touchings" by hand and by weapon, it says, "calls to mind the unavailing defense of the person who 'persistently denied that he had laid hands upon a priest, for he had only cudgelled and kicked him.'" Ibid. But the quip exposes the majority's bind. To get where it wishes to go, the majority not only must rework the rules found in the cases on which it relies, it must also abandon their rationale. The debt-collection cases treated the "laying on of hands" as a sign of *possession.* Maybe the possession was more "constructive" or even fictional than "actual." But the idea was that someone who stood next to a debtor and laid hands on him could theoretically exercise a degree of control over his person. Common law courts never said the same of bailiffs who fired arrows at debtors, shot them with firearms, or cudgeled them as they ran away. Such conduct might have amounted to a *battery,* but it was never deemed sufficient to constitute an *arrest.* Doubtless that's why when a tax collector shot a man in the eye with a (supposedly unavailable) firearm in 1682, the man sued the officer for "assault, battery, and wounding" — *not* false imprisonment. See *Dickenson,* Jones, T., at 205, 84 Eng. Rep., at 1218–1219.

The majority implores us to study the common law history of arrests. But almost immediately, the majority realizes it cannot find what it seeks in the history of criminal arrests. So it is forced to disinter a long-abandoned mere-touch rule from civil bankruptcy practice. Then it must import that rule into the criminal law. And because even that isn't enough to do the work it wishes done, the majority must jettison both the laying on of hands requirement and the rationale that sustained it. All of which leaves us confusing seizures with their attempts and arrests with batteries.

The common law offers a vast legal library. Like any other, it must be used thoughtfully. We have no business wandering about and randomly grabbing volumes off the shelf, plucking out passages we like, scratching out bits we don't, all before pasting our own new pastiche into the U. S. Reports. That does not respect legal history; it rewrites it.

If text and history pose challenges for the majority, so do this Court's precedents. . . .

In Terry v. Ohio, 392 U.S. 1 (1968), the Court explained that "*[o]nly* when the officer, by means of physical force or show of authority, has in some way restrained the liberty of a citizen may we conclude that a 'seizure' has occurred." Id., at 19, n. 16 (emphasis added). The restraint of liberty *Terry* referred to was "interference" with a person's "freedom of movement." United States v. Jacobsen, 466 U.S. 109, 113, n. 5 (1984).

As the Court put it in Brower v. County of Inyo, 489 U.S. 593 (1989), a decision issued just two years before *Hodari D.*: "It is clear, in other words, that a Fourth Amendment seizure" occurs "only when there is a governmental termination of freedom of movement through means intentionally applied." 489 U.S., at 597 (emphasis deleted).

Rather than follow these teachings, the majority disparages them. After highlighting (multiple times) that Justice Scalia authored *Hodari D.*'s dicta, the majority turns about and faults his opinion for the Court in *Brower* for "improperly eras[ing] the distinction between seizures by *control* and seizures by *force*." The majority continues on to blame other of our decisions, too, for "hav[ing] not always been attentive" to this supposedly fundamental distinction. Ibid. But this Court has not been "[in]attentive" to a fundamental Fourth Amendment distinction for over two centuries, let alone sought to "erase" it. In truth, the majority's "distinction" is a product of its own invention. This Court has always recognized that *how* seizures take place can differ. Some may take place after a show of authority, others by the application of force, still others after a polite request. But to *be* a "seizure," the same result has always been required: An officer must acquire possession.

IV

If text, history, and precedent cannot explain today's result, what can? The majority seems to offer a clue when it promises its new rule will help us "avoi[d] . . . line-drawing problems." Any different standard, the majority worries, would be "difficult to apply."

But if efficiency in judicial administration is the explanation, it is a troubling one. Surely our role as interpreters of the Constitution isn't to make life easier for ourselves. Nor, for that matter, has the majority even tried to show that the traditional possession rule—in use "[f]rom the time of the founding," *Hodari D.*, 499 U.S., at 624—has proven unreasonably difficult to administer. Everyone agrees, too, that the possession rule will continue to govern when it comes to the seizures of objects and persons through a show of authority. So, rather than simplify things, the majority's new rule for "mere touch" seizures promises only to add another layer of complexity to the law.

Even within its field of operation, the majority's rule seems destined to underdeliver on its predicted efficiencies. The majority tells us that its new test requires an "objective intent to restrain." But what qualifies is far from clear. The majority assures us that a "tap on the shoulder to get one's attention will rarely exhibit such an intent." Suppose, though, the circumstances "objectively" indicate that the tap was "intended" to secure a person's attention for a minute, a quarter hour, or longer. Would that be enough?

Then there's the question what kind of "touching" will suffice. Imagine that, with an objective intent to detain a suspect, officers deploy pepper spray that enters a suspect's lungs as he sprints away. Does the application of the pepper spray count? Suppose that, intending to capture a fleeing suspect, officers detonate flash-bang grenades that are so loud they damage the suspect's eardrum, even though he manages to run off. Or imagine an officer shines a laser into a suspect's eyes to get him to stop, but the suspect is able to drive away with now-damaged retinas. Are these "touchings"? What about an officer's bullet that shatters the driver's windshield, a piece of which cuts her as she speeds away? Maybe the officer didn't touch the suspect, but he set in motion a series of events that yielded a touching. Does that count? While assuring us that its new rule will prove easy to administer, the majority refuses to confront its certain complications. Lower courts and law enforcement won't have that luxury.

If efficiency cannot explain today's decision, what's left? Maybe it is an impulse that individuals like Ms. Torres *should* be able to sue for damages. Sometimes police shootings are justified, but other times they cry out for a remedy. The majority seems to give voice to this sentiment when it disparages the traditional possession rule as "artificial" and promotes its alternative as more sensitive to "personal security" and "new" policing realities. It takes pains to explain, too, that its new rule will provide greater protection for personal "privacy" interests, which we're told make up the "essence" of the Fourth Amendment.

But tasked only with applying the Constitution's terms, we have no authority to posit penumbras of "privacy" and "personal security" and devise whatever rules we think might best serve the Amendment's "essence." The Fourth Amendment allows this Court to protect against specific governmental actions—unreasonable searches and seizures of persons, houses, papers, and effects—and that is the limit of our license. Besides, it's hard to see why we should stretch to invent a new remedy here. Ms. Torres had ready-made claims for assault and battery under New Mexico law to test the officers' actions. The only reason this case comes before us under § 1983 and the Fourth Amendment rather than before a New Mexico court under state tort law seems to be that Ms. Torres (or her lawyers) missed the State's two-year statutory filing deadline. . . .

Nor, if we are honest, does today's decision promise much help to anyone else. Like Ms. Torres, many seeking to sue officers will be able to bring state tort claims. Even for those whose only recourse is a federal lawsuit, the majority's new rule seems likely to accomplish little. This Court has already said that a remedy lies under § 1983 and the Fourteenth Amendment for police conduct that "shocks the conscience." County of Sacramento v. Lewis, 523 U.S. 833, 840, 845–847 (1998). At the same time, qualified immunity poses a daunting hurdle for those seeking to recover for less egregious police behavior. In our own case, Ms. Torres has yet to clear that bar and still faces it on remand. So, at the end of it all, the majority's new rule will help only those who (1) lack a state-law remedy, (2) evade custody, (3) after some physical contact by the police, (4) where the contact was sufficient to show an objective intent to restrain, (5) and where the police acted "unreasonably" in light of clearly established law, (6) but the police conduct was *not* "conscience shocking." With qualification heaped on qualification, that can describe only a vanishingly small number of cases. . . .

In the face of these concerns, the majority replies by denying their relevance. It says there is "no call" to "surmise" that its decision rests on anything beyond an "analysis of the common law of arrest." But there is no surmise about it. The majority itself tells us that its decision is *also* justified by the need to "avoi[d] . . . line-drawing problems," protect "personal security," and advance the "privacy" interests that form the "essence" of the Fourth Amendment. Having invoked these sundry considerations, it's hard to see how the majority might disown them.

* * *

To rule as it does, the majority must endow the term "seizure" with two different meanings at the same time. It must disregard the dominant rule of the common law. It must disparage this Court's existing case law for erasing distinctions that never existed. It cannot even guarantee that its new rule will offer great efficiencies or meaningfully vindicate the penumbral promises it supposes. Instead, we are asked to skip from one snippet to another, finally landing on a long-abandoned debt-collection practice that must be reengineered to do the work the majority wishes done. Our final destination confuses a battery for a seizure and an attempted seizure with its completion. All this is miles from where the standard principles of interpretation lead and just as far from the Constitution's original meaning. And for what? A new rule that may seem tempting at first blush, but that offers those like Ms. Torres little more than false hope in the end.

Respectfully, I dissent.

NOTES AND QUESTIONS

1. Isn't *Torres* an interesting study in the use of the common law and its history to interpret the Fourth Amendment? Recall that in Note 1 after *Hodari D.*, we noted the Court's use of the common law to define the meaning of a seizure and suggested that it was in tension with modern precedents like *Katz*, which expanded the reach of the Fourth Amendment to encompass the "seizure" of sound from a telephone booth. Does *Torres*, following but also building on the analysis in *Hodari D.*, suggest that the common law approach to interpretation can *also* expand the reach of the Fourth Amendment in important ways?

2. But does *Torres* at the same time suggest that the common law does not necessarily generate clear answers to important questions? We will consider this point again, after reading Atwater v. Lago Vista, 532 U.S. 318 (2001), at page 600, on the subject whether the Fourth Amendment forbids a warrantless arrest for a minor criminal offense. But isn't it already clear, from *Torres*, that reasonable minds can differ on the proper application of the common law to modern problems? In fact, doesn't the dissent make a strong case that the majority is distorting the common law history? What does *this* tell us, about an approach to Fourth Amendment interpretation that has grown increasingly important in the 21st century?

3. One thing about the common law approach that is probably undeniable: Time spent perusing the common law in a judicial opinion will not be spent considering the contemporary merits of one constitutional rule, as opposed to another. What about this, in light of the statement, in the opening pages of this chapter, that "[i]t is not too much to say that the Fourth Amendment functions as a kind of tort law for the police, the chief source of legal regulation of criminal law enforcement"? See supra at page 315. To the extent that the Supreme Court embraces a common law approach to Fourth Amendment interpretation, is the Court likely to do better, or worse, in regulating police conduct?

4. What about the rule adopted by the majority, considered on its own terms? As already suggested, it appears to flow naturally enough from *Hodari D.*'s conclusion that the application of physical force with intent to subdue is sufficient to constitute a seizure, whether effective at stopping an individual or not. But given that Torres, as the dissent points out, already had available to her at least one cause of action, is the addition of a Fourth Amendment claim important, as a regulatory matter? Is it sufficient to ensure that police use firearms appropriately and with restraint? You will have occasion in these materials to repeatedly consider a point made by Professor Amsterdam over 40 years ago that the "great American

vacuum" of "subconstitutional" controls on police conduct has been a significant barrier to placing effective constraints on police. See Anthony G.
Amsterdam, Perspectives on the Fourth Amendment, 58 Minn. L. Rev. 349,
380 (1974). Could it be that decisions like *Torres* risk deflecting attention
from (or even the development of) these subconstitutional controls? You
may wish to consider this question again after studying the materials later
in the chapter on the Fourth Amendment regulation of police use of force.

C. *Justifying Searches and Seizures*

3. Justifying Searches and Seizures Without Warrants

a. *Exigent Circumstances*

Insert the following Note after Note 3 on page 487:

4. The Court recently returned to these questions in Lange v. California,
594 U.S. ___ (2021). A California highway patrol officer pursued Lange
into his driveway and attached garage after Lange failed to pull over when
the officer signaled to Lange, who was playing loud music and honking his
horn. Lange ultimately was charged with a misdemeanor DUI based upon
evidence collected in his garage. California argued that the warrantless
pursuit into Lange's home was permissible because the officer had probable cause to arrest him, but the Court disagreed and rejected a categorical
rule that pursuit of a suspected misdemeanant justifies warrantless entry
into the home without some additional factor, such as imminent harm to
others, destruction of evidence, or escape from the home. Chief Justice
Roberts wrote separately, concurring in the Court's judgment and noting
prior Court decisions explicitly rejecting the notion that certain kinds of
police action are unreasonable simply because a case involves a minor
offense. The Chief Justice also expressed concern regarding the administrability of the *Lange* Court's approach.

Consider in this regard Atwater v. Lago Vista, 532 U.S. 318 (2001), the
main case at page 600. In *Atwater,* a case involving the constitutionality
of a custodial arrest for a fine-only seatbelt violation, Justice Souter wrote
for the majority that a bright-line rule focused on probable cause for
arrest—no matter the lack of seriousness of the offense—was necessary
to support the administrability of law enforcement rules. The *Lange* Court
rejected precisely this approach.

Do you think that the constitutional law of arrest requires more "bright-line" rules than warrantless entry into the home? Is there a different consideration at play? Perhaps the *Lange* Court considered Lange's conduct at issue here to be less serious than Gail Atwater's seatbelt-law violation? It seems the Court is grappling with how best to address and constrain police discretion in a world of proliferating public order and low-level offenses. Keep *Lange* in mind as you read the materials at pages 600-625 that further address this topic.

Insert the following Note and main case after Note 13 on page 491:

14. Finally, consider the Court's latest word on the scope of police authority to, in particular, enter a home in service of community caretaking ends unrelated or, at best, marginally related to traditional law enforcement. In *Caniglia v. Strom*, the Court rejected the notion that there is a "standalone" Fourth Amendment rule emanating from Cady v. Dombrowski, 413 U.S. 433 (1973), that permits police to enter homes in service of a myriad of community caretaking purposes. At the same time, isn't the Court careful to make clear that there are numerous circumstances in which entry may be justified under the Fourth Amendment, albeit via an analysis less simplistic than that employed by the Court of Appeals? What does *Caniglia* tell us about the scope of police authority in this context today?

CANIGLIA v. STROM
Certiorari to the United States Court of Appeals for the First Circuit
593 U.S. ___ (2021)

JUSTICE THOMAS delivered the opinion of the Court.

Decades ago, this Court held that a warrantless search of an impounded vehicle for an unsecured firearm did not violate the Fourth Amendment. Cady v. Dombrowski, 413 U.S. 433 (1973). In reaching this conclusion, the Court observed that police officers who patrol the "public highways" are often called to discharge noncriminal "community caretaking functions," such as responding to disabled vehicles or investigating accidents. Id., at 441. The question today is whether *Cady*'s acknowledgment of these "caretaking" duties creates a standalone doctrine that justifies warrantless searches and seizures in the home. It does not.

I

During an argument with his wife at their Rhode Island home, Edward Caniglia (petitioner) retrieved a handgun from the bedroom, put it on the dining room table, and asked his wife to "shoot [him] now and get it over with." She declined, and instead left to spend the night at a hotel. The next morning, when petitioner's wife discovered that she could not reach him by telephone, she called the police (respondents) to request a welfare check.

Respondents accompanied petitioner's wife to the home, where they encountered petitioner on the porch. Petitioner spoke with respondents and confirmed his wife's account of the argument, but denied that he was suicidal. Respondents, however, thought that petitioner posed a risk to himself or others. They called an ambulance, and petitioner agreed to go to the hospital for a psychiatric evaluation—but only after respondents allegedly promised not to confiscate his firearms. Once the ambulance had taken petitioner away, however, respondents seized the weapons. Guided by petitioner's wife—whom they allegedly misinformed about his wishes—respondents entered the home and took two handguns.

Petitioner sued, claiming that respondents violated the Fourth Amendment when they entered his home and seized him and his firearms without a warrant. The District Court granted summary judgment to respondents, and the First Circuit affirmed solely on the ground that the decision to remove petitioner and his firearms from the premises fell within a "community caretaking exception" to the warrant requirement. Citing this Court's statement in *Cady* that police officers often have non-criminal reasons to interact with motorists on "public highways," the First Circuit extrapolated a freestanding community-caretaking exception that applies to both cars and homes. Accordingly, the First Circuit saw no need to consider whether anyone had consented to respondents' actions; whether these actions were justified by "exigent circumstances"; or whether any state law permitted this kind of mental-health intervention. . . . We granted certiorari.

II

The Fourth Amendment protects "[t]he right of the people to be secure in their persons, houses, papers, and effects, against unreasonable searches and seizures." The "'very core'" of this guarantee is "'the right of a man to retreat into his own home and there be free from unreasonable governmental intrusion.'" Florida v. Jardines, 569 U. S. 1, 6 (2013).

To be sure, the Fourth Amendment does not prohibit all unwelcome intrusions "on private property," ibid. — only "unreasonable" ones. We have thus recognized a few permissible invasions of the home and its curtilage. Perhaps most familiar, for example, are searches and seizures pursuant to a valid warrant. We have also held that law enforcement officers may enter private property without a warrant when certain exigent circumstances exist, including the need to "'render emergency assistance to an injured occupant or to protect an occupant from imminent injury.'" Kentucky v. King, 563 U.S. 452, 460, 470 (2011); see also Brigham City v. Stuart, 547 U.S. 398, 403-404 (2006) (listing other examples of exigent circumstances). And, of course, officers may generally take actions that "'any private citizen might do'" without fear of liability. E.g., Jardines, 569 U.S., at 8 (approaching a home and knocking on the front door).

The First Circuit's "community caretaking" rule, however, goes beyond anything this Court has recognized. The decision below assumed that respondents lacked a warrant or consent, and it expressly disclaimed the possibility that they were reacting to a crime. The court also declined to consider whether any recognized exigent circumstances were present because respondents had forfeited the point. Nor did it find that respondents' actions were akin to what a private citizen might have had authority to do if petitioner's wife had approached a neighbor for assistance instead of the police.

Neither the holding nor logic of *Cady* justified that approach. True, *Cady* also involved a warrantless search for a firearm. But the location of that search was an impounded vehicle — not a home — "'a constitutional difference'" that the opinion repeatedly stressed. In fact, *Cady* expressly contrasted its treatment of a vehicle already under police control with a search of a car "parked adjacent to the dwelling place of the owner." [413 U.S., at 446-448 (citing Coolidge v. New Hampshire, 403 U.S. 443 (1971))].

Cady's unmistakable distinction between vehicles and homes also places into proper context its reference to "community caretaking." This quote comes from a portion of the opinion explaining that the "frequency with which . . . vehicle[s] can become disabled or involved in . . . accident[s] on public highways" often requires police to perform noncriminal "community caretaking functions," such as providing aid to motorists. 413 U.S. at 441. But, this recognition that police officers perform many civic tasks in modern society was just that — a recognition that these tasks exist, and not an open-ended license to perform them anywhere.

* * *

What is reasonable for vehicles is different from what is reasonable for homes. *Cady* acknowledged as much, and this Court has repeatedly "declined to expand the scope of . . . exceptions to the warrant requirement to permit warrantless entry into the home." Collins [v. Virginia, 584 U.S. ___, ___ (2018).] We thus vacate the judgment below and remand for further proceedings consistent with this opinion. . . .

CHIEF JUSTICE ROBERTS, with whom JUSTICE BREYER joins, concurring.

Fifteen years ago, this Court unanimously recognized that "[t]he role of a peace officer includes preventing violence and restoring order, not simply rendering first aid to casualties." Brigham City v. Stuart, 547 U.S. 398, 406 (2006). A warrant to enter a home is not required, we explained, when there is a "need to assist persons who are seriously injured or threatened with such injury." Id., at 403; see also Michigan v. Fisher, 558 U. S. 45, 49 (2009) (*per curiam*) (warrantless entry justified where "there was an objectively reasonable basis for believing that medical assistance was needed, or persons were in danger"). Nothing in today's opinion is to the contrary, and I join it on that basis.

JUSTICE ALITO, concurring.

I join the opinion of the Court but write separately to explain my understanding of the Court's holding and to highlight some important questions that the Court does not decide.

1. The Court holds—and I entirely agree—that there is no special Fourth Amendment rule for a broad category of cases involving "community caretaking." As I understand the term, it describes the many police tasks that go beyond criminal law enforcement. These tasks vary widely, and there is no clear limit on how far they might extend in the future. The category potentially includes any non-law-enforcement work that a community chooses to assign, and because of the breadth of activities that may be described as community caretaking, we should not assume that the Fourth Amendment's command of reasonableness applies in the same way to everything that might be viewed as falling into this broad category. . . .

2. While there is no overarching "community caretaking" doctrine, it does not follow that all searches and seizures conducted for non-law-enforcement purposes must be analyzed under precisely the same Fourth Amendment rules developed in criminal cases. Those rules may or may not be appropriate for use in various non-criminal-law-enforcement contexts. We do not decide that issue today.

3. This case falls within one important category of cases that could be viewed as involving community caretaking: conducting a search or seizure

for the purpose of preventing a person from committing suicide. Assuming that petitioner did not voluntarily consent to go with the officers for a psychological assessment, he was seized and thus subjected to a serious deprivation of liberty. But was this warrantless seizure "reasonable"? We have addressed the standards required by due process for involuntary commitment to a mental treatment facility, see Addington v. Texas, 441 U.S. 418, 427 (1979); see also O'Connor v. Donaldson, 422 U.S. 563, 574-576 (1975); Foucha v. Louisiana, 504 U.S. 71, 75-77, 83 (1992), but we have not addressed Fourth Amendment restrictions on seizures like the one that we must assume occurred here, i.e., a short-term seizure conducted for the purpose of ascertaining whether a person presents an imminent risk of suicide. Every State has laws allowing emergency seizures for psychiatric treatment, observation, or stabilization, but these laws vary in many respects, including the categories of persons who may request the emergency action, the reasons that can justify the action, the necessity of a judicial proceeding, and the nature of the proceeding. Mentioning these laws only in passing, petitioner asked us to render a decision that could call features of these laws into question. The Court appropriately refrains from doing so.

4. This case also implicates another body of law that petitioner glossed over: the so-called "red flag" laws that some States are now enacting. These laws enable the police to seize guns pursuant to a court order to prevent their use for suicide or the infliction of harm on innocent persons. . . . Provisions of red flag laws may be challenged under the Fourth Amendment, and those cases may come before us. Our decision today does not address these issues.

5. One additional category of cases should be noted: those involving warrantless, nonconsensual searches of a home for the purpose of ascertaining whether a resident is in urgent need of medical attention and cannot summon help. At oral argument, the Chief Justice posed a question that highlighted this problem. He imagined a situation in which neighbors of an elderly woman call the police and express concern because the woman had agreed to come over for dinner at 6 p.m., but by 8 p.m., had not appeared or called even though she was never late for anything. The woman had not been seen leaving her home, and she was not answering the phone. Nor could the neighbors reach her relatives by phone. If the police entered the home without a warrant to see if she needed help, would that violate the Fourth Amendment?

Petitioner's answer was that it would. Indeed, he argued, even if 24 hours went by, the police still could not lawfully enter without a warrant. If the situation remained unchanged for several days, he suggested, the police might be able to enter after obtaining "a warrant for a missing person."

The Chief Justice's question concerns an important real-world problem. Today, more than ever, many people, including many elderly persons, live alone. Many elderly men and women fall in their homes, or become incapacitated for other reasons, and unfortunately, there are many cases in which such persons cannot call for assistance. In those cases, the chances for a good recovery may fade with each passing hour. So in the Chief Justice's imaginary case, if the elderly woman was seriously hurt or sick and the police heeded petitioner's suggestion about what the Fourth Amendment demands, there is a fair chance she would not be found alive. This imaginary woman may have regarded her house as her castle, but it is doubtful that she would have wanted it to be the place where she died alone and in agony.

Our current precedents do not address situations like this. We have held that the police may enter a home without a warrant when there are "exigent circumstances." Payton v. New York, 445 U.S. 573, 590 (1980). But circumstances are exigent only when there is not enough time to get a warrant, see Missouri v. McNeely, 569 U.S. 141, 149 (2013); Michigan v. Tyler, 436 U.S. 499, 509 (1978), and warrants are not typically granted for the purpose of checking on a person's medical condition. Perhaps States should institute procedures for the issuance of such warrants, but in the meantime, courts may be required to grapple with the basic Fourth Amendment question of reasonableness.

6. The three categories of cases discussed above are simply illustrative. Searches and seizures conducted for other non-law-enforcement purposes may arise and may present their own Fourth Amendment issues. Today's decision does not settle those questions.

In sum, the Court properly rejects the broad "community caretaking" theory on which the decision below was based. The Court's decision goes no further, and on that understanding, I join the opinion in full.

JUSTICE KAVANAUGH, concurring.

I join the Court's opinion in full. I write separately to underscore and elaborate on the Chief Justice's point that the Court's decision does not prevent police officers from taking reasonable steps to assist those who are inside a home and in need of aid. . . .

[T]he Fourth Amendment protects the "right of the people to be secure in their persons, houses, papers, and effects, against unreasonable searches and seizures." As the constitutional text establishes, the "ultimate touchstone of the Fourth Amendment is reasonableness." Riley v. California,

573 U.S. 373, 381 (2014). The Court has said that a warrant supported by probable cause is ordinarily required for law enforcement officers to enter a home. See U.S. Const., Amdt. 4. But drawing on common-law analogies and a commonsense appraisal of what is "reasonable," the Court has cognized various situations where a warrant is not required. For example, the exigent circumstances doctrine allows officers to enter a home without a warrant in certain situations, including: to fight a fire and investigate its cause; to prevent the imminent destruction of evidence; to engage in hot pursuit of a fleeing felon or prevent a suspect's escape; to address a threat to the safety of law enforcement officers or the general public; to render emergency assistance to an injured occupant; or to protect an occupant who is threatened with serious injury.

Over the years, many courts, like the First Circuit in this case, have relied on what they have labeled a "community caretaking" doctrine to allow warrantless entries into the home for a non-investigatory purpose, such as to prevent a suicide or to conduct a welfare check on an older individual who has been out of contact. But as the Court today explains, any such standalone community caretaking doctrine was primarily devised for searches of cars, not homes.

But this Fourth Amendment issue is more labeling than substance. The Court's Fourth Amendment case law already recognizes the exigent circumstances doctrine, which allows an officer to enter a home without a warrant if the "exigencies of the situation make the needs of law enforcement so compelling that the warrantless search is objectively reasonable under the Fourth Amendment." Brigham City [v. Stuart, 547 U.S. 398, 403 (2006)]. As relevant here, one such recognized "exigency" is the "need to assist persons who are seriously injured or threatened with such injury." The Fourth Amendment allows officers to enter a home if they have "an objectively reasonable basis for believing" that such help is needed, and if the officers' actions inside the home are reasonable under the circumstances. *Brigham City*, 547 U. S., at 406.

This case does not require us to explore all the contours of the exigent circumstances doctrine as applied to emergency-aid situations because the officers here disclaimed reliance on that doctrine. But to avoid any confusion going forward, I think it important to briefly describe how the doctrine applies to some heartland emergency-aid situations.

As Chief Judge Livingston has cogently explained, although this doctrinal area does not draw much attention from courts or scholars, "municipal police spend a good deal of time responding to calls about missing persons, sick neighbors, and premises left open at night." Livingston, Police, Community Caretaking, and the Fourth Amendment, 1998 U. Chi. Leg.

Forum 261, 263 (1998). And as she aptly noted, "the responsibility of police officers to search for missing persons, to mediate disputes, and to aid the ill or injured has never been the subject of serious debate; nor has" the "responsibility of police to provide services in an emergency." Id., at 302.

Consistent with that reality, the Court's exigency precedents, as I read them, permit warrantless entries when police officers have an objectively reasonable basis to believe that there is a current, ongoing crisis for which it is reasonable to act now.

The officers do not need to show that the harm has already occurred or is mere moments away, because knowing that will often be difficult if not impossible in cases involving, for example, a person who is currently suicidal or an elderly person who has been out of contact and may have fallen. If someone is at risk of serious harm and it is reasonable for officers to intervene now, that is enough for the officers to enter.

A few (non-exhaustive) examples illustrate the point.

Suppose that a woman calls a healthcare hotline or 911 and says that she is contemplating suicide, that she has firearms in her home, and that she might as well die. The operator alerts the police, and two officers respond by driving to the woman's home. They knock on the door but do not receive a response. May the officers enter the home? Of course.

The exigent circumstances doctrine applies because the officers have an "objectively reasonable basis" for believing that an occupant is "seriously injured or threatened with such injury." Id., at 400, 403; cf. [City and County of San Francisco v.] Sheehan, 575 U.S. [600], 612 (officers could enter the room of a mentally ill person who had locked herself inside with a knife). After all, a suicidal individual in such a scenario could kill herself at any moment. The Fourth Amendment does not require officers to stand idly outside as the suicide takes place.

Consider another example. Suppose that an elderly man is uncharacteristically absent from Sunday church services and repeatedly fails to answer his phone throughout the day and night. A concerned relative calls the police and asks the officers to perform a wellness check. Two officers drive to the man's home. They knock but receive no response. May the officers enter the home? Of course.

Again, the officers have an "objectively reasonable basis" for believing that an occupant is "seriously injured or threatened with such injury." *Brigham City*, 547 U.S. at 400, 403. Among other possibilities, the elderly man may have fallen and hurt himself, a common cause of death or serious injury for older individuals. The Fourth Amendment does not prevent the officers from entering the home and checking on the man's well-being.

To be sure, courts, police departments, and police officers alike must take care that officers' actions in those kinds of cases are reasonable under the circumstances. But both of those examples and others as well, such as cases involving unattended young children inside a home, illustrate the kinds of warrantless entries that are perfectly constitutional under the exigent circumstances doctrine, in my view.

With those observations, I join the Court's opinion in full.

NOTES AND QUESTIONS

1. Did the Court in the last few paragraphs of its opinion essentially limit *Cady* to its facts — namely, the search of an "impounded vehicle" that was "already under police control?" If the holding in *Cady* is limited to the situation in *Cady* itself, does that suggest that its reference to "community caretaking" no longer establishes any broader authority to search even cars, much less homes, in service of community caretaking ends?

2. At the same time, don't at least four Justices take pains to make clear that the majority is not seeking to draw into question the authority of police to respond to a range of circumstances presenting an immediate need to help those in need of assistance — the ill, the suicidal, those unable to take care of themselves — whether or not they are inside a home? And doesn't the majority reiterate that law enforcement officers may enter a home whenever exigent circumstances exist — including the need to render emergency assistance to the injured or to protect an occupant from imminent injury?

3. But is this articulation of the exigent circumstances exception sufficiently robust to authorize police to do a wellness check in search of a missing elderly relative? What does "imminence" mean in this context? What counts as an "emergency"?

Note that, in his concurrence, Chief Justice Roberts alludes to Brigham City v. Stuart, 547 U.S. 398 (2006), but without reference to the "imminence" language to be found in that opinion. And Justice Alito makes clear that, in his view, courts after *Caniglia* must "grapple with the basic Fourth Amendment question of reasonableness" in assessing various types of non-law-enforcement purposes that might require search or seizure within a home. Alito notes the limitations of the traditional exigent circumstances exception in this context — that the exception applies only when there is not enough time to get a warrant, but warrants do not typically issue to check on the wellbeing of elderly relatives. Is Alito correct that the majority opinion "does not settle" the question of whether entry for such purposes is nevertheless reasonable?

4. Finally, the Court in *Caniglia* observes that police may generally take actions that private citizens might take, without fear of liability. Is this a source of guidance, in determining the scope of police authority to undertake wellness checks and the like?

Add the following Note after Note 3 on page 578:

4. In Kansas v. Glover, 589 U.S. ___ (2020), the Court addressed whether a police officer had reasonable suspicion to infer that the person driving a motor vehicle was the owner. The officer had run a routine check of the vehicle's license plate and received a database "hit" that the registered owner of the vehicle had a revoked driver's license. The officer stopped the vehicle, and the driver (who did turn out to be the owner) ultimately was charged with "driving as a habitual violator."

Justice Thomas, writing for eight members of the Court, concluded that the officer's judgment that the owner and the driver were probably the same person was a reasonable "commonsense inference," although he did not explain *why* he felt that was the case. Justice Sotomayor, the lone dissenter, argued that the majority's approach departed from the Court's well-established requirement that reasonable suspicion should be based only on an officer's established training or experience. Here, she asserted, the officer's reliance on "common sense" basically flipped the burden of proof that requires the police to establish proper grounds for reasonable suspicion.

Justice Sotomayor may well be correct, if the lower courts read the case broadly, but it is important to note that both the majority and Justices Kagan and Ginsburg (in concurrence) took pains to emphasize the narrow scope of the holding—specifically, the fact that the owner of the car had a prior history of ignoring traffic laws, as well as the complete absence of any other facts in the record that might have caused the officer to question whether the driver of the car might actually be someone other than the owner.

D.   Reasonableness and Police Use of Force

Add the following paragraph at the end of Note 4 on page 716:

One important variable in determining whether a police officer's actions are reasonable is the law itself that governs excessive force. If a factual situation has been found to permit or to deny the use of a certain level of force under a certain set of facts, presumably that should be a significant variable for the police to take into account when deciding how to respond to an encounter, as well as an important variable in analyzing the objective reasonableness of an action. That, in turn, suggests that the police should be instructed as to the substantive content of the law of excessive force. It turns out that they apparently are not so instructed. See Joanna C. Schwartz, Qualified Immunity's Boldest Lie, available online at https://papers.ssrn.com/sol3/papers.cfm?abstract_id=3659540, reporting the results of a study of police training and education materials and concluding that "officers are not notified of the facts and holdings of cases that clearly establish the law . . . . Instead, officers are taught the general principles of *Graham* and *Garner* and then are told to apply those principles in the widely varying circumstances that come their way." This lack of instruction on the caselaw affects not only the reasonableness of police use of force, but also the good faith exception to the exclusionary rule, and even more deeply whether the entire exclusionary rule regime is sensible. If police officers do not know the law, it is difficult to see how exclusionary rulings will deter them.

Chapter 7

The Fifth Amendment

D. Police Interrogation

3. The Consequences of a *Miranda* Violation

Add the following paragraph at the end of Note 5 on page 1002:

Or is it, according to the Court, *Miranda* that is the problem? To resolve the issue left open in *Chavez*, the Court returned to the status of the *Miranda* warnings in Vega v. Tekoh, 597 U.S. ___ (2022). The question in *Tekoh* was "whether a violation of the *Miranda* rules provides a basis for a claim under §1983. We hold that it does not." The Court noted the peculiar state of *Miranda* jurisprudence but explicitly held that the violation of *Miranda's* requirements is not a violation of the Fifth Amendment. The Court went no further but did not demonstrate much enthusiasm for the overall holding in *Miranda*, noting in footnote 5:

> Whether this Court has the authority to create constitutionally based pro- phylactic rules that bind both federal and state courts has been the subject of debate among jurists and commentators. . . . But that is what the Court did in *Miranda*, and we do not disturb that decision in any way. Rather, we accept it on its own terms, and for the purpose of deciding this case, we follow its rationale.

Reading Supreme Court tea leaves is a tricky business, but consider the implication of Dobbs v. Jackson Women's Health Organization, 597 U.S. ___ (2022), overruling Roe v. Wade, 410 U.S. 113 (2022), in part because of the Court's view that a right to an abortion lacks any grounding in nor- mal interpretive constitutional methodologies. If that signals an increasing willingness on the part of the Court to reconsider cases without a solid basis in traditional constitutional analysis or based on the idea of a "living Constitution," might *Miranda* someday be in its crosshairs?

PART FOUR

THE ADJUDICATION PROCESS

Chapter 10

Pretrial Screening and the Grand Jury

C. Grand Jury Investigations

Add the following Note after Note 3 on page 1123:

4. As noted earlier, the Grand Jury Clause of the Fifth Amendment is not incorporated against the States, and so the use of grand juries in state proceedings varies widely. But the scope of the subpoena power is often comparable to that in the federal system. In Trump v. Vance, 591 U.S. ___ (2020), a New York state grand jury subpoenaed some financial records of President Donald Trump, who resisted on the grounds that that the Supremacy Clause gives a sitting president absolute immunity from complying with state subpoenas; the President argued that having to respond to state subpoenas would inevitably interfere with the performance of his Article II duties. The Supreme Court, by 7-2, rejected the argument. Although the Court recognized that the power to investigate a sitting president could in some circumstances lead to harassment by political opponents, a categorical rule forbidding these subpoenas is not required. The Court noted that, among other things, grand juries are prohibited from engaging in "arbitrary fishing expeditions" (citing *R. Enterprises*, supra), and that federal courts have the power to intervene in state court cases "in those cases where the District Court properly finds that the state proceeding is motivated by a desire to harass or is conducted in bad faith." The Court also rejected the Solicitor General's more limited argument that a subpoena directed at a sitting president needed to demonstrate a specific showing of need.

Is the potential for federal courts to intervene and quash subpoenas under the *R. Enterprises* test really sufficient to protect a president from political harassment? Even if courts are more willing than usual to act when it is the president who is being investigated, isn't the need to respond to subpoenas and litigate their validity itself a disruption that could interfere with the proper functioning of the executive branch?

Chapter 11

The Scope of the Prosecution

B. Venue

2. Changes of Venue

Add the following paragraph at the end of Note 3 on page 1191:

The Court reiterated this point in United States v. Tsarnaev, 595 U.S. ___ (2022), which involved the conviction and death sentence of one of the men responsible for the bombing at the 2013 Boston Marathon, which killed three and left hundreds injured. The trial in the Boston federal courthouse attracted intense media coverage, and during voir dire, the defense requested that prospective jurors be asked to list the facts they had already learned about the case. The district judge declined to ask this "unfocused" and "unguided" question, but the First Circuit found that this failure to inquire was, in part, a basis for vacating the death sentence. The Supreme Court reversed the court of appeals and found that this decision not to ask the question at voir dire was well within the district judge's discretion. Quoting *Skilling*, the Court observed that "[w]hen pretrial publicity is at issue, primary reliance on the judgment of the trial court makes [especially] good sense. After all, the judge sits in the locale where the publicity is said to have had its effect and may base her evaluation on her own perception of the depth and extent of news stories that might influence a juror."

Chapter 14

The Jury and the Criminal Trial

A. The Right to a Trial by Jury

In Note 4 on pages 1346-1347, delete the sentence that begins at the bottom of page 1346 (starting with "Nearly . . .") and carries over to the top of page 1347. In addition, replace the last paragraph of Note 4 on page 1347 with the following:

Despite the longstanding unanimity rule for federal juries, for nearly four decades the states were constitutionally permitted to proceed with non-unanimous juries as the result of an odd 4-1-4 split on the Supreme Court in the case of Apodaca v. Oregon, 406 U.S. 404 (1972). However, *Apodaca* was finally overruled by Ramos v. Louisiana, 590 U.S. ___ (2020); thus, the Sixth Amendment now requires unanimous jury verdicts in both state and federal criminal cases (but note that, per Edwards v. Vannoy, 592 U.S. ___ (2021), the *Ramos* decision does not apply retroactively on federal habeas; see infra at page 1681).

C. The Defendant's Trial Rights

2. The Confrontation Clause

a. The *Crawford* Revolution

Add the following before the first sentence of Crawford v. Washington on page 1394:

JUSTICE SCALIA delivered the opinion of the Court.

In Note 4 on page 1416, insert the following paragraph between the existing second and third paragraphs:

Consider, in this regard, the Court's decision in Hemphill v. New York, 595 U.S. ___ (2022), where the issue was whether a defendant could lose his confrontation rights if he "opened the door" to the hearsay testimony. Hemphill was charged with murder, and at trial he tried to shift the blame to a third party. In response, the State introduced parts of the third-party's earlier guilty plea allocution, despite defendant's objection that, because the third party was now unavailable, the statements were not subject to cross examination. The State argued that these statements were not barred by the Confrontation Clause because the defendant opened the door to this evidence by putting the third party's culpability in issue, and that admission of the statements was necessary to present a complete picture for the factfinder and thus to preserve the truth-seeking function of the trial. By an 8-1 vote, the Supreme Court rejected these arguments, reiterating that *Crawford* demanded a certain *process* for establishing the reliability of testimony—subjecting the statements to cross-examination—and that this was true even if the trial judge found that the testimony was "necessary" to correct a "misleading impression" that defendant himself had created. The Court admonished that "the role of the trial judge is not, for Confrontation Clause purposes, to weigh the reliability or credibility of testimonial hearsay evidence; it is to ensure that the Constitution's procedures for testing the reliability of that evidence are followed."

PART FIVE

POST-TRIAL PROCEEDINGS

Chapter 15

Sentencing

A. Introduction to Sentencing

Delete the last two sentences of Note 5 on page 1514. Add the following paragraph at the end of Note 5 on page 1515:

In Jones v. Mississippi, 592 U.S. ___ (2021), the Court held that *Miller* and *Montgomery* do *not* require a sentencing judge to make a finding (either explicit or implicit) that a juvenile is "permanently incorrigible" (i.e., not amenable to rehabilitation) before sentencing the juvenile to life without parole—thereby severely curtailing the impact of those decisions and suggesting that the Court has no current intention to further limit the punishments imposed on juveniles. In an impassioned dissent, Justice Sotomayor (joined by Justices Breyer and Kagan) accused the majority of "overrul[ing] precedent without even acknowledging it is doing so"; the end result, according to Sotomayor, is that "far too many juvenile offenders will be sentenced to die in prison." For his part, Justice Thomas, concurring in the judgment, agreed that the majority "adopts a strained reading of *Montgomery*," and suggested that the Court should have simply overruled that decision.

Chapter 16

Double Jeopardy

C. Double Jeopardy and the "Dual Sovereignty" Doctrine

Add the following paragraph at the end of Note 5 on page 1617:

And, in Denezpi v. United States, 596 U.S. ___ (2022), the Court held that the Double Jeopardy Clause does *not* bar successive prosecutions of distinct offenses arising from a single act, even if a single sovereign prosecutes them. The case involved a member of the Navajo Nation who was initially charged by an officer from the federal Bureau of Indian Affairs with a crime under the Ute Mountain Ute Code, and then later by a federal grand jury with a crime under the federal Major Crimes Act. The Court explained that even though the federal government was behind both of the *prosecutions*, the *offenses* that were charged derived from distinct sovereign sources—and thus fit within the dual sovereignty doctrine.

Chapter 17

Appellate and Collateral Review

A. Appellate Review

5. Prejudice and Harmless Error

Add the following paragraph at the end of Note 9 on page 1650:

In Davis v. United States, 589 U.S. ___ (2020), a unanimous *per curiam* Court held that "plain error" review under Rule 52(b) potentially applies to all unpreserved errors—factual as well as legal—which meant that the Fifth Circuit's practice of refusing even to consider unpreserved factual errors must be overturned.

B. Collateral Review

2. The Nature and Purposes of Federal Habeas

Add the following footnote 6(a) at the end of the second-to-last paragraph on page 1655:

6(a). The second *Teague* exception was later eliminated in Edwards v. Vannoy, 592 U.S. ___ (2021); see infra at page 1681.

3. Procedural Issues in Federal Habeas

c. Procedural Default

Add the following paragraph at the end of Note 4 on page 1678:

Adding to the confusion, the Court in Shinn v. Martinez Ramirez, 596 U.S. ___ (2022), held that *Martinez* does *not* allow a habeas petitioner to supplement the evidentiary record as it was developed in the state court—even if the deficiencies in that state-court record resulted from the ineffectiveness of state post-conviction counsel. The Court noted that the strict limitations on evidentiary hearings in federal habeas come from AEDPA itself, not from judicial decisions, and thus are not subject to judicial modification. See infra, at page 1680, subsection (f). As a practical matter, *Martinez Ramirez* severely limits *Martinez*, because most ineffective-assistance-of-trial-counsel claims require additional factual development beyond the trial record—and such development is unlikely to have happened if state post-conviction counsel failed even to raise the claim.

d. Successive Petitions and Abuse of the Writ

Add the following paragraph at the end of Subsection (d) on page 1680:

In Banister v. Davis, 590 U.S. ___ (2020), the Court held that a motion filed under Rule 59(e) asking a district court to alter or amend its judgment—which must be filed within 28 days of the entry of the judgment, without possibility of an extension—does not constitute a "second or successive" habeas petition that triggers the restrictions of 28 U.S.C. §2244.

4. What Law Applies?

Replace the first paragraph of this subsection on page 1681 with the following:

We have already seen that under AEDPA, federal habeas courts, as a general matter, can apply only federal constitutional law that was clearly established, by the decisions of the U.S. Supreme Court, as of the time of the state court's final decision. New rules of constitutional law generally do not apply; in this sense, AEDPA has codified the rule of Teague v. Lane (1989), a pre-AEDPA decision that has been repeatedly reaffirmed by the Court since AEDPA. See supra, at page 1655.

In *Teague,* the Court recognized two exceptions to the basic rule of non-retroactivity of "new rules" in federal habeas: (1) new "substantive" rules that make it unconstitutional to criminalize certain kinds of conduct, and (2) "watershed" rules of criminal procedure that are "implicit in the concept of ordered liberty." But in Edwards v. Vannoy, 592 U.S. ___ (2021), the second of these *Teague* exceptions was eliminated.

Edwards involved the retroactivity of Ramos v. Louisiana, 590 U.S. ___ (2020) (see page 1347), the decision holding that the Sixth Amendment requires jury verdicts in state criminal cases to be unanimous. According to the *Edwards* Court (per Justice Kavanaugh), *Ramos*—while "momentous and consequential"—was no more so than other previous decisions like Mapp v. Ohio (1961) (see page 318), Miranda v. Arizona (1966) (see page 897), Duncan v. Louisiana (1968) (see page 71), Crawford v. Washington (2004) (see page 1394), and Batson v. Kentucky (1986) (see page 1360), all of which were held non-retroactive in federal habeas. Thus *Ramos* likewise "does not apply retroactively on federal collateral review." The majority opinion, however, did not stop there:

> If landmark and historic criminal procedure decisions—including *Mapp, Miranda, Duncan, Crawford, Batson,* and now *Ramos*—do not apply retroactively on federal collateral review, how can any additional new rules of criminal procedure apply retroactively on federal collateral review? At this point, some 32 years after *Teague,* we think the only candid answer is that none can—that is, no new rules of criminal procedure can satisfy the watershed exception. We cannot responsibly continue to suggest otherwise to litigants and courts. . . . [T]he purported exception has become an empty promise.
>
> Continuing to articulate a theoretical exception that never actually applies in practice offers false hope to defendants, distorts the law, misleads judges, and wastes the resources of defense counsel, prosecutors, and courts. Moreover, no one can reasonably rely on an exception that is non-existent in practice, so no reliance interests can be affected by forthrightly acknowledging reality. It is time—probably long past time—to make explicit what has become increasingly apparent to bench and bar over the last 32 years: New procedural rules do not apply retroactively on federal collateral review. . . .
>
> [N]o *stare decisis* values would be served by continuing to indulge the fiction that *Teague's* purported watershed exception endures. . . .

Edwards, 592 U.S., at ___. In other words, with respect to the rules of constitutional criminal procedure in federal habeas cases, "old law" is the only law that applies.

But this is not the only limitation on the law that applies in federal habeas cases.

5. Prejudice and Harmless Error

Add the following Note after Note 2 on page 1698:

In Brown v. Davenport, 596 U.S. ___ (2022), the Court held that federal habeas courts must apply *both* the harmless error standard of *Brecht and* the heightened "unreasonable" standard of review created by AEDPA before granting relief to a state prisoner in federal habeas. The Court rejected the petitioner's argument that satisfying *Brecht* (which the lower court had held he had) automatically satisfies the AEDPA standard of review, noting that *Brecht* is about whether "a habeas court *itself* harbors grave doubt" about the verdict, whereas AEDPA's standard is based on whether "*every* fairminded jurist would agree that an error was prejudicial."

Selected Rules and Statutes

Federal Rules of Criminal Procedure

Rule 1. Scope; Definitions

(a) **Scope.**

(1) In General. These rules govern the procedure in all criminal proceedings in the United States district courts, the United States courts of appeals, and the Supreme Court of the United States.

(2) State or Local Judicial Officer. When a rule so states, it applies to a proceeding before a state or local judicial officer.

(3) Territorial Courts. These rules also govern the procedure in all criminal proceedings in the following courts:

(A) the district court of Guam;

(B) the district court for the Northern Mariana Islands, except as otherwise provided by law; and

(C) the district court of the Virgin Islands, except that the prosecution of offenses in that court must be by indictment or information as otherwise provided by law.

(4) Removed Proceedings. Although these rules govern all proceedings after removal from a state court, state law governs a dismissal by the prosecution.

(5) Excluded Proceedings. Proceedings not governed by these rules include:

(A) the extradition and rendition of a fugitive;

(B) a civil property forfeiture for violating a federal statute;

(C) the collection of a fine or penalty;

(D) a proceeding under a statute governing juvenile delinquency to the extent the procedure is inconsistent with the statute, unless Rule 20(d) provides otherwise;

(E) a dispute between seamen under 22 U.S.C. §§256-258; and

(F) a proceeding against a witness in a foreign country under 28 U.S.C. §1784.

(b) Definitions. The following definitions apply to these rules:

(1) "Attorney for the government" means:

(A) the Attorney General or an authorized assistant;

(B) a United States attorney or an authorized assistant;

(C) when applicable to cases arising under Guam law, the Guam Attorney General or other person whom Guam law authorizes to act in the matter; and

(D) any other attorney authorized by law to conduct proceedings under these rules as a prosecutor.

(2) "Court" means a federal judge performing functions authorized by law.

(3) "Federal judge" means:

(A) a justice or judge of the United States as these terms are defined in 28 U.S.C. §451;

(B) a magistrate judge; and

(C) a judge confirmed by the United States Senate and empowered by statute in any commonwealth, territory, or possession to perform a function to which a particular rule relates.

(4) "Judge" means a federal judge or a state or local judicial officer.

(5) "Magistrate judge" means a United States magistrate judge as defined in 28 U.S.C. §§631-639.

(6) "Oath" includes an affirmation.

(7) "Organization" is defined in 18 U.S.C. §18.

(8) "Petty offense" is defined in 18 U.S.C. §19.

(9) "State" includes the District of Columbia, and any commonwealth, territory, or possession of the United States.

(10) "State or local judicial officer" means:

(A) a state or local officer authorized to act under 18 U.S.C. §3041; and

(B) a judicial officer empowered by statute in the District of Columbia or in any commonwealth, territory, or possession to perform a function to which a particular rule relates.

(11) "Telephone" means any technology for transmitting live electronic voice communication.

(12) "Victim" means a "crime victim" as defined in 18 U.S.C. §3771(e).

(c) Authority of a Justice or Judge of the United States. When these rules authorize a magistrate judge to act, any other federal judge may also act.

Rule 2. Interpretation

These rules are to be interpreted to provide for the just determination of every criminal proceeding, to secure simplicity in procedure and fairness in administration, and to eliminate unjustifiable expense and delay.

Rule 3. The Complaint

The complaint is a written statement of the essential facts constituting the offense charged. Except as provided in Rule 4.1, it must be made under oath before a magistrate judge or, if none is reasonably available, before a state or local judicial officer.

Rule 4. Arrest Warrant or Summons on a Complaint

(a) **Issuance.** If the complaint or one or more affidavits filed with the complaint establish probable cause to believe that an offense has been committed and that the defendant committed it, the judge must issue an arrest warrant to an officer authorized to execute it. At the request of an attorney for the government, the judge must issue a summons, instead of a warrant, to a person authorized to serve it. A judge may issue more than one warrant or summons on the same complaint. If an individual defendant fails to appear in response to a summons, a judge may, and upon request of an attorney for the government must, issue a warrant. If an organizational defendant fails to appear in response to a summons, a judge may take any action authorized by United States law.

(b) **Form.**

(1) Warrant. A warrant must:

(A) contain the defendant's name or, if it is unknown, a name or description by which the defendant can be identified with reasonable certainty;

(B) describe the offense charged in the complaint;

(C) command that the defendant be arrested and brought without unnecessary delay before a magistrate judge or, if none is reasonably available, before a state or local judicial officer; and

(D) be signed by a judge.

(2) Summons. A summons must be in the same form as a warrant except that it must require the defendant to appear before a magistrate judge at a stated time and place.

(c) Execution or Service, and Return.

(1) By Whom. Only a marshal or other authorized officer may execute a warrant. Any person authorized to serve a summons in a federal civil action may serve a summons.

(2) Location. A warrant may be executed, or a summons served, within the jurisdiction of the United States or anywhere else a federal statute authorizes an arrest. A summons to an organization under Rule 4(c)(3)(D) may also be served at a place not within a judicial district of the United States.

(3) Manner.

(A) A warrant is executed by arresting the defendant. Upon arrest, an officer possessing the original or a duplicate original warrant must show it to the defendant. If the officer does not possess the warrant, the officer must inform the defendant of the warrant's existence and of the offense charged and, at the defendant's request, must show the original or a duplicate original warrant to the defendant as soon as possible.

(B) A summons is served on an individual defendant:

(i) by delivering a copy to the defendant personally; or

(ii) by leaving a copy at the defendant's residence or usual place of abode with a person of suitable age and discretion residing at that location and by mailing a copy to the defendant's last known address.

(C) A summons is served on an organization in a judicial district of the United States by delivering a copy to an officer, to a managing or general agent, or to another agent appointed or legally authorized to receive service of process. If the agent is one authorized by statute and the statute so requires, a copy must also be mailed to the organization.

(D) A summons is served on an organization not within a judicial district of the United States:

(i) by delivering a copy, in a manner authorized by the foreign jurisdiction's law, to an officer, to a managing or general agent, or to an agent appointed or legally authorized to receive service of process; or

(ii) by any other means that gives notice, including one that is:

(a) stipulated by the parties;

(b) undertaken by a foreign authority in response to a letter rogatory, a letter of request, or a request submitted under an applicable international agreement; or

(c) permitted by an applicable international agreement.

(4) Return.

(A) After executing a warrant, the officer must return it to the judge before whom the defendant is brought in accordance with Rule 5. The officer may do so by reliable electronic means. At the request of an attorney for the government, an unexecuted warrant must be brought back to and canceled by a magistrate judge or, if none is reasonably available, by a state or local judicial officer.

(B) The person to whom a summons was delivered for service must return it on or before the return day.

(C) At the request of an attorney for the government, a judge may deliver an unexecuted warrant, an unserved summons, or a copy of the warrant or summons to the marshal or other authorized person for execution or service.

(d) Warrant by Telephone or Other Reliable Electronic Means. In accordance with Rule 4.1, a magistrate judge may issue a warrant or summons based on information communicated by telephone or other reliable electronic means.

Rule 4.1. Complaint, Warrant, or Summons by Telephone or Other Reliable Electronic Means

(a) In General. A magistrate judge may consider information communicated by telephone or other reliable electronic means when reviewing a complaint or deciding whether to issue a warrant or summons.

(b) Procedures. If a magistrate judge decides to proceed under this rule, the following procedures apply:

(1) Taking Testimony Under Oath. The judge must place under oath — and may examine — the applicant and any person on whose testimony the application is based.

(2) Creating a Record of the Testimony and Exhibits.

(A) Testimony Limited to Attestation. If the applicant does no more than attest to the contents of a written affidavit submitted by reliable electronic means, the judge must acknowledge the attestation in writing on the affidavit.

(B) Additional Testimony or Exhibits. If the judge considers additional testimony or exhibits, the judge must:

(i) have the testimony recorded verbatim by an electronic recording device, by a court reporter, or in writing;

(ii) have any recording or reporter's notes transcribed, have the transcription certified as accurate, and file it;

(iii) sign any other written record, certify its accuracy, and file it; and

(iv) make sure that the exhibits are filed.

(3) Preparing a Proposed Duplicate Original of a Complaint, Warrant, or Summons. The applicant must prepare a proposed duplicate original of a complaint, warrant, or summons, and must read or otherwise transmit its contents verbatim to the judge.

(4) Preparing an Original Complaint, Warrant, or Summons. If the applicant reads the contents of the proposed duplicate original, the judge must enter those contents into an original complaint, warrant, or summons. If the applicant transmits the contents by reliable electronic means, the transmission received by the judge may serve as the original.

(5) Modification. The judge may modify the complaint, warrant, or summons. The judge must then:

(A) transmit the modified version to the applicant by reliable electronic means; or

(B) file the modified original and direct the applicant to modify the proposed duplicate original accordingly.

(6) Issuance. To issue the warrant or summons, the judge must:

(A) sign the original documents;

(B) enter the date and time of issuance on the warrant or summons; and

(C) transmit the warrant or summons by reliable electronic means to the applicant or direct the applicant to sign the judge's name and enter the date and time on the duplicate original.

(c) Suppression Limited. Absent a finding of bad faith, evidence obtained from a warrant issued under this rule is not subject to suppression on the ground that issuing the warrant in this manner was unreasonable under the circumstances.

Rule 5.   Initial Appearance

(a) In General.

(1) Appearance Upon an Arrest.

(A) A person making an arrest within the United States must take the defendant without unnecessary delay before a magistrate judge, or before a state or local judicial officer as Rule 5(c) provides, unless a statute provides otherwise.

(B) A person making an arrest outside the United States must take the defendant without unnecessary delay before a magistrate judge, unless a statute provides otherwise.

(2) Exceptions.

(A) An officer making an arrest under a warrant issued upon a complaint charging solely a violation of 18 U.S.C. §1073 need not comply with this rule if:

(i) the person arrested is transferred without unnecessary delay to the custody of appropriate state or local authorities in the district of arrest; and

(ii) an attorney for the government moves promptly, in the district where the warrant was issued, to dismiss the complaint.

(B) If a defendant is arrested for violating probation or supervised release, Rule 32.1 applies.

(C) If a defendant is arrested for failing to appear in another district, Rule 40 applies.

(3) Appearance Upon a Summons. When a defendant appears in response to a summons under Rule 4, a magistrate judge must proceed under Rule 5(d) or (e), as applicable.

(b) Arrest Without a Warrant. If a defendant is arrested without a warrant, a complaint meeting Rule 4(a)'s requirement of probable cause must be promptly filed in the district where the offense was allegedly committed.

(c) Place of Initial Appearance; Transfer to Another District.

(1) Arrest in the District Where the Offense Was Allegedly Committed. If the defendant is arrested in the district where the offense was allegedly committed:

(A) the initial appearance must be in that district; and

(B) if a magistrate judge is not reasonably available, the initial appearance may be before a state or local judicial officer.

(2) Arrest in a District Other Than Where the Offense Was Allegedly Committed. If the defendant was arrested in a district other than where the offense was allegedly committed, the initial appearance must be:

(A) in the district of arrest; or

(B) in an adjacent district if:

(i) the appearance can occur more promptly there; or

(ii) the offense was allegedly committed there and the initial appearance will occur on the day of arrest.

(3) Procedures in a District Other Than Where the Offense Was Allegedly Committed. If the initial appearance occurs in a district other than where the offense was allegedly committed, the following procedures apply:

(A) the magistrate judge must inform the defendant about the provisions of Rule 20;

(B) if the defendant was arrested without a warrant, the district court where the offense was allegedly committed must first issue a warrant before the magistrate judge transfers the defendant to that district;

(C) the magistrate judge must conduct a preliminary hearing if required by Rule 5.1;

(D) the magistrate judge must transfer the defendant to the district where the offense was allegedly committed if:

(i) the government produces the warrant, a certified copy of the warrant, or a reliable electronic form of either; and

(ii) the judge finds that the defendant is the same person named in the indictment, information, or warrant; and

(E) when a defendant is transferred and discharged, the clerk must promptly transmit the papers and any bail to the clerk in the district where the offense was allegedly committed.

(4) Procedure for Persons Extradited to the United States. If the defendant is surrendered to the United States in accordance with a request for the defendant's extradition, the initial appearance must be in the district (or one of the districts) where the offense is charged.

(d) Procedure in a Felony Case.

(1) Advice. If the defendant is charged with a felony, the judge must inform the defendant of the following:

(A) the complaint against the defendant, and any affidavit filed with it;

(B) the defendant's right to retain counsel or to request that counsel be appointed if the defendant cannot obtain counsel;

(C) the circumstances, if any, under which the defendant may secure pretrial release;

(D) any right to a preliminary hearing;

(E) the defendant's right not to make a statement, and that any statement made may be used against the defendant; and

(F) that a defendant who is not a United States citizen may request that an attorney for the government or a federal law enforcement official notify a consular officer from the defendant's country of nationality that the defendant has been arrested—but that even without the defendant's request, a treaty or other international agreement may require consular notification.

(2) Consulting with Counsel. The judge must allow the defendant reasonable opportunity to consult with counsel.

(3) Detention or Release. The judge must detain or release the defendant as provided by statute or these rules.

(4) Plea. A defendant may be asked to plead only under Rule 10.

(e) **Procedure in a Misdemeanor Case.** If the defendant is charged with a misdemeanor only, the judge must inform the defendant in accordance with Rule 58(b)(2).

(f) **Reminder of Prosecutorial Obligation.**

(1) In General. In all criminal proceedings, on the first scheduled court date when both prosecutor and defense counsel are present, the judge shall issue an oral and written order to prosecution and defense counsel that confirms the disclosure obligation of the prosecutor under Brady v. Maryland, 373 U.S. 83 (1963) and its progeny, and the possible consequences of violating such order under applicable law.

(2) Formation of Order. Each judicial council in which a district court is located shall promulgate a model order for the purpose of paragraph (1) that the court may use as it determines is appropriate.

(g) **Video Teleconferencing.** Video teleconferencing may be used to conduct an appearance under this rule if the defendant consents.

Rule 5.1. Preliminary Hearing

(a) **In General.** If a defendant is charged with an offense other than a petty offense, a magistrate judge must conduct a preliminary hearing unless:

(1) the defendant waives the hearing;

(2) the defendant is indicted;

(3) the government files an information under Rule 7(b) charging the defendant with a felony;

(4) the government files an information charging the defendant with a misdemeanor; or

(5) the defendant is charged with a misdemeanor and consents to trial before a magistrate judge.

(b) **Selecting a District.** A defendant arrested in a district other than where the offense was allegedly committed may elect to have the preliminary hearing conducted in the district where the prosecution is pending.

(c) Scheduling. The magistrate judge must hold the preliminary hearing within a reasonable time, but no later than 14 days after the initial appearance if the defendant is in custody and no later than 21 days if not in custody.

(d) Extending the Time. With the defendant's consent and upon a showing of good cause—taking into account the public interest in the prompt disposition of criminal cases—a magistrate judge may extend the time limits in Rule 5.1(c) one or more times. If the defendant does not consent, the magistrate judge may extend the time limits only on a showing that extraordinary circumstances exist and justice requires the delay.

(e) Hearing and Finding. At the preliminary hearing, the defendant may cross-examine adverse witnesses and may introduce evidence but may not object to evidence on the ground that it was unlawfully acquired. If the magistrate judge finds probable cause to believe an offense has been committed and the defendant committed it, the magistrate judge must promptly require the defendant to appear for further proceedings.

(f) Discharging the Defendant. If the magistrate judge finds no probable cause to believe an offense has been committed or the defendant committed it, the magistrate judge must dismiss the complaint and discharge the defendant. A discharge does not preclude the government from later prosecuting the defendant for the same offense.

(g) Recording the Proceedings. The preliminary hearing must be recorded by a court reporter or by a suitable recording device. A recording of the proceeding may be made available to any party upon request. A copy of the recording and a transcript may be provided to any party upon request and upon any payment required by applicable Judicial Conference regulations.

(h) Producing a Statement.

(1) In General. Rule 26.2(a)-(d) and (f) applies at any hearing under this rule, unless the magistrate judge for good cause rules otherwise in a particular case.

(2) Sanctions for Not Producing a Statement. If a party disobeys a Rule 26.2 order to deliver a statement to the moving party, the magistrate judge must not consider the testimony of a witness whose statement is withheld.

Rule 6.   The Grand Jury

(a) Summoning a Grand Jury.

(1) In General. When the public interest so requires, the court must order that one or more grand juries be summoned. A grand jury

must have 16 to 23 members, and the court must order that enough legally qualified persons be summoned to meet this requirement.

(2) Alternate Jurors. When a grand jury is selected, the court may also select alternate jurors. Alternate jurors must have the same qualifications and be selected in the same manner as any other juror. Alternate jurors replace jurors in the same sequence in which the alternates were selected. An alternate juror who replaces a juror is subject to the same challenges, takes the same oath, and has the same authority as the other jurors.

(b) Objection to the Grand Jury or to a Grand Juror.

(1) Challenges. Either the government or a defendant may challenge the grand jury on the ground that it was not lawfully drawn, summoned, or selected, and may challenge an individual juror on the ground that the juror is not legally qualified.

(2) Motion to Dismiss an Indictment. A party may move to dismiss the indictment based on an objection to the grand jury or on an individual juror's lack of legal qualification, unless the court has previously ruled on the same objection under Rule 6(b)(1). The motion to dismiss is governed by 28 U.S.C. §1867(e). The court must not dismiss the indictment on the ground that a grand juror was not legally qualified if the record shows that at least 12 qualified jurors concurred in the indictment.

(c) Foreperson and Deputy Foreperson. The court will appoint one juror as the foreperson and another as the deputy foreperson. In the foreperson's absence, the deputy foreperson will act as the foreperson. The foreperson may administer oaths and affirmations and will sign all indictments. The foreperson—or another juror designated by the foreperson—will record the number of jurors concurring in every indictment and will file the record with the clerk, but the record may not be made public unless the court so orders.

(d) Who May Be Present.

(1) While the Grand Jury Is in Session. The following persons may be present while the grand jury is in session: attorneys for the government, the witness being questioned, interpreters when needed, and a court reporter or an operator of a recording device.

(2) During Deliberations and Voting. No person other than the jurors, and any interpreter needed to assist a hearing-impaired or speech-impaired juror, may be present while the grand jury is deliberating or voting.

(e) Recording and Disclosing the Proceedings.

(1) Recording the Proceedings. Except while the grand jury is deliberating or voting, all proceedings must be recorded by a

court reporter or by a suitable recording device. But the validity of a prosecution is not affected by the unintentional failure to make a recording. Unless the court orders otherwise, an attorney for the government will retain control of the recording, the reporter's notes, and any transcript prepared from those notes.

(2) Secrecy.

(A) No obligation of secrecy may be imposed on any person except in accordance with Rule 6(e)(2)(B).

(B) Unless these rules provide otherwise, the following persons must not disclose a matter occurring before the grand jury:

(i) a grand juror;

(ii) an interpreter;

(iii) a court reporter;

(iv) an operator of a recording device;

(v) a person who transcribes recorded testimony;

(vi) an attorney for the government; or

(vii) a person to whom disclosure is made under Rule 6(e)(3)(A)(ii) or (iii).

(3) Exceptions.

(A) Disclosure of a grand-jury matter—other than the grand jury's deliberations or any grand juror's vote—may be made to:

(i) an attorney for the government for use in performing that attorney's duty;

(ii) any government personnel—including those of a state, state subdivision, Indian tribe, or foreign government—that an attorney for the government considers necessary to assist in performing that attorney's duty to enforce federal criminal law; or

(iii) a person authorized by 18 U.S.C. §3322.

(B) A person to whom information is disclosed under Rule 6(e)(3)(A)(ii) may use that information only to assist an attorney for the government in performing that attorney's duty to enforce federal criminal law. An attorney for the government must promptly provide the court that impaneled the grand jury with the names of all persons to whom a disclosure has been made, and must certify that the attorney has advised those persons of their obligation of secrecy under this rule.

(C) An attorney for the government may disclose any grand-jury matter to another federal grand jury.

(D) An attorney for the government may disclose any grand-jury matter involving foreign intelligence, counterintelligence (as defined in 50 U.S.C. §3003), or foreign intelligence information (as defined in Rule 6(e)(3)(D)(iii)) to any federal law enforcement, intelligence, protective, immigration, national defense, or national security official to assist the official receiving the information in the performance of that official's duties. An attorney for the government may also disclose any grand-jury matter involving, within the United States or elsewhere, a threat of attack or other grave hostile acts of a foreign power or its agent, a threat of domestic or international sabotage or terrorism, or clandestine intelligence gathering activities by an intelligence service or network of a foreign power or by its agent, to any appropriate federal, state, state subdivision, Indian tribal, or foreign government official, for the purpose of preventing or responding to such threat or activities.

(i) Any official who receives information under Rule 6(e)(3)(D) may use the information only as necessary in the conduct of that person's official duties subject to any limitations on the unauthorized disclosure of such information. Any state, state subdivision, Indian tribal, or foreign government official who receives information under Rule 6(e)(3)(D) may use the information only in a manner consistent with any guidelines issued by the Attorney General and the Director of National Intelligence.

(ii) Within a reasonable time after disclosure is made under Rule 6(e)(3)(D), an attorney for the government must file, under seal, a notice with the court in the district where the grand jury convened stating that such information was disclosed and the departments, agencies, or entities to which the disclosure was made.

(iii) As used in Rule 6(e)(3)(D), the term "foreign intelligence information" means:

(a) information, whether or not it concerns a United States person, that relates to the ability of the United States to protect against—

- actual or potential attack or other grave hostile acts of a foreign power or its agent;
- sabotage or international terrorism by a foreign power or its agent; or
- clandestine intelligence activities by an intelligence service or network of a foreign power or by its agent; or

(b) information, whether or not it concerns a United States person, with respect to a foreign power or foreign territory that relates to—

- the national defense or the security of the United States; or
- the conduct of the foreign affairs of the United States.

(E) The court may authorize disclosure—at a time, in a manner, and subject to any other conditions that it directs—of a grand-jury matter:

(i) preliminarily to or in connection with a judicial proceeding;

(ii) at the request of a defendant who shows that a ground may exist to dismiss the indictment because of a matter that occurred before the grand jury;

(iii) at the request of the government, when sought by a foreign court or prosecutor for use in an official criminal investigation;

(iv) at the request of the government if it shows that the matter may disclose a violation of State, Indian tribal, or foreign criminal law, as long as the disclosure is to an appropriate state, state-subdivision, Indian tribal, or foreign government official for the purpose of enforcing that law; or

(v) at the request of the government if it shows that the matter may disclose a violation of military criminal law under the Uniform Code of Military Justice, as long as the disclosure is to an appropriate military official for the purpose of enforcing that law.

(F) A petition to disclose a grand-jury matter under Rule 6(e)(3)(E)(i) must be filed in the district where the grand jury convened. Unless the hearing is ex parte—as it may be when the government is the petitioner—the petitioner must serve the petition on, and the court must afford a reasonable opportunity to appear and be heard to:

(i) an attorney for the government;

(ii) the parties to the judicial proceeding; and

(iii) any other person whom the court may designate.

(G) If the petition to disclose arises out of a judicial proceeding in another district, the petitioned court must transfer the petition to the other court unless the petitioned court can reasonably determine whether disclosure is proper. If the petitioned court decides to transfer, it must send to the transferee court the material sought to be disclosed, if feasible, and a written evaluation of the need for continued grand-jury secrecy. The transferee court must afford those persons identified in Rule 6(e)(3)(F) a reasonable opportunity to appear and be heard.

(4) Sealed Indictment. The magistrate judge to whom an indictment is returned may direct that the indictment be kept secret until the defendant is in custody or has been released pending trial. The

clerk must then seal the indictment, and no person may disclose the indictment's existence except as necessary to issue or execute a warrant or summons.

(5) Closed Hearing. Subject to any right to an open hearing in a contempt proceeding, the court must close any hearing to the extent necessary to prevent disclosure of a matter occurring before a grand jury.

(6) Sealed Records. Records, orders, and subpoenas relating to grand-jury proceedings must be kept under seal to the extent and as long as necessary to prevent the unauthorized disclosure of a matter occurring before a grand jury.

(7) Contempt. A knowing violation of Rule 6, or of any guidelines jointly issued by the Attorney General and the Director of National Intelligence under Rule 6, may be punished as a contempt of court.

(f) Indictment and Return. A grand jury may indict only if at least 12 jurors concur. The grand jury—or its foreperson or deputy foreperson—must return the indictment to a magistrate judge in open court. To avoid unnecessary cost or delay, the magistrate judge may take the return by video teleconference from the court where the grand jury sits. If a complaint or information is pending against the defendant and 12 jurors do not concur in the indictment, the foreperson must promptly and in writing report the lack of concurrence to the magistrate judge.

(g) Discharging the Grand Jury. A grand jury must serve until the court discharges it, but it may serve more than 18 months only if the court, having determined that an extension is in the public interest, extends the grand jury's service. An extension may be granted for no more than 6 months, except as otherwise provided by statute.

(h) Excusing a Juror. At any time, for good cause, the court may excuse a juror either temporarily or permanently, and if permanently, the court may impanel an alternate juror in place of the excused juror.

(i) "Indian Tribe" Defined. "Indian tribe" means an Indian tribe recognized by the Secretary of the Interior on a list published in the Federal Register under 25 U.S.C. §479a-1.

Rule 7.   The Indictment and the Information

(a) When Used.

(1) Felony. An offense (other than criminal contempt) must be prosecuted by an indictment if it is punishable:

(A) by death; or

(B) by imprisonment for more than one year.

(2) Misdemeanor. An offense punishable by imprisonment for one year or less may be prosecuted in accordance with Rule 58(b)(1).

(b) Waiving Indictment. An offense punishable by imprisonment for more than one year may be prosecuted by information if the defendant—in open court and after being advised of the nature of the charge and of the defendant's rights—waives prosecution by indictment.

(c) Nature and Contents.

(1) In General. The indictment or information must be a plain, concise, and definite written statement of the essential facts constituting the offense charged and must be signed by an attorney for the government. It need not contain a formal introduction or conclusion. A count may incorporate by reference an allegation made in another count. A count may allege that the means by which the defendant committed the offense are unknown or that the defendant committed it by one or more specified means. For each count, the indictment or information must give the official or customary citation of the statute, rule, regulation, or other provision of law that the defendant is alleged to have violated. For purposes of an indictment referred to in section 3282 of title 18, United States Code, for which the identity of the defendant is unknown, it shall be sufficient for the indictment to describe the defendant as an individual whose name is unknown, but who has a particular DNA profile, as that term is defined in section 3282.

(2) Citation Error. Unless the defendant was misled and thereby prejudiced, neither an error in a citation nor a citation's omission is a ground to dismiss the indictment or information or to reverse a conviction.

(d) Surplusage. Upon the defendant's motion, the court may strike surplusage from the indictment or information.

(e) Amending an Information. Unless an additional or different offense is charged or a substantial right of the defendant is prejudiced, the court may permit an information to be amended at any time before the verdict or finding.

(f) Bill of Particulars. The court may direct the government to file a bill of particulars. The defendant may move for a bill of particulars before or within 14 days after arraignment or at a later time if the court permits. The government may amend a bill of particulars subject to such conditions as justice requires.

Rule 8.   Joinder of Offenses or Defendants

(a) **Joinder of Offenses.** The indictment or information may charge a defendant in separate counts with two or more offenses if the offenses charged—whether felonies or misdemeanors or both—are of the same or similar character, or are based on the same act or transaction, or are connected with or constitute parts of a common scheme or plan.

(b) **Joinder of Defendants.** The indictment or information may charge two or more defendants if they are alleged to have participated in the same act or transaction, or in the same series of acts or transactions, constituting an offense or offenses. The defendants may be charged in one or more counts together or separately. All defendants need not be charged in each count.

Rule 9.   Arrest Warrant or Summons on an Indictment or Information

(a) **Issuance.** The court must issue a warrant—or at the government's request, a summons—for each defendant named in an indictment or named in an information if one or more affidavits accompanying the information establish probable cause to believe that an offense has been committed and that the defendant committed it. The court may issue more than one warrant or summons for the same defendant. If a defendant fails to appear in response to a summons, the court may, and upon request of an attorney for the government must, issue a warrant. The court must issue the arrest warrant to an officer authorized to execute it or the summons to a person authorized to serve it.

(b) **Form.**

(1) Warrant. The warrant must conform to Rule 4(b)(1) except that it must be signed by the clerk and must describe the offense charged in the indictment or information.

(2) Summons. The summons must be in the same form as a warrant except that it must require the defendant to appear before the court at a stated time and place.

(c) Execution or Service; Return; Initial Appearance.

(1) Execution or Service.

(A) The warrant must be executed or the summons served as provided in Rule 4(c)(1), (2), and (3).

(B) The officer executing the warrant must proceed in accordance with Rule 5(a)(1).

(2) Return. A warrant or summons must be returned in accordance with Rule 4(c)(4).

(3) Initial Appearance. When an arrested or summoned defendant first appears before the court, the judge must proceed under Rule 5.

Rule 10.   Arraignment

(a) In General. An arraignment must be conducted in open court and must consist of:

(1) ensuring that the defendant has a copy of the indictment or information;

(2) reading the indictment or information to the defendant or stating to the defendant the substance of the charge; and then

(3) asking the defendant to plead to the indictment or information.

(b) Waiving Appearance. A defendant need not be present for the arraignment if:

(1) the defendant has been charged by indictment or misdemeanor information;

(2) the defendant, in a written waiver signed by both the defendant and defense counsel, has waived appearance and has affirmed that the defendant received a copy of the indictment or information and that the plea is not guilty; and

(3) the court accepts the waiver.

(c) Video Teleconferencing. Video teleconferencing may be used to arraign a defendant if the defendant consents.

Rule 11.   Pleas

(a) Entering a Plea.

(1) In General. A defendant may plead not guilty, guilty, or (with the court's consent) nolo contendere.

(2) Conditional Plea. With the consent of the court and the government, a defendant may enter a conditional plea of guilty or nolo contendere, reserving in writing the right to have an appellate

court review an adverse determination of a specified pretrial motion. A defendant who prevails on appeal may then withdraw the plea.

(3) Nolo Contendere Plea. Before accepting a plea of nolo contendere, the court must consider the parties' views and the public interest in the effective administration of justice.

(4) Failure to Enter a Plea. If a defendant refuses to enter a plea or if a defendant organization fails to appear, the court must enter a plea of not guilty.

(b) Considering and Accepting a Guilty or Nolo Contendere Plea.

(1) Advising and Questioning the Defendant. Before the court accepts a plea of guilty or nolo contendere, the defendant may be placed under oath and the court must address the defendant personally in open court. During this address, the court must inform the defendant of, and determine that the defendant understands, the following:

(A) the government's right, in a prosecution for perjury or false statement, to use against the defendant any statement that the defendant gives under oath;

(B) the right to plead not guilty, or having already so pleaded, to persist in that plea;

(C) the right to a jury trial;

(D) the right to be represented by counsel—and, if necessary, have the court appoint counsel—at trial and at every other stage of the proceeding;

(E) the right at trial to confront and cross-examine adverse witnesses, to be protected from compelled self-incrimination, to testify and present evidence, and to compel the attendance of witnesses;

(F) the defendant's waiver of these trial rights if the court accepts a plea of guilty or nolo contendere;

(G) the nature of each charge to which the defendant is pleading;

(H) any maximum possible penalty, including imprisonment, fine, and term of supervised release;

(I) any mandatory minimum penalty;

(J) any applicable forfeiture;

(K) the court's authority to order restitution;

(L) the court's obligation to impose a special assessment;

(M) in determining a sentence, the court's obligation to calculate the applicable sentencing-guideline range and to consider that range, possible departures under the Sentencing Guidelines, and other sentencing factors under 18 U.S.C. §3553(a);

(N) the terms of any plea-agreement provision waiving the right to appeal or to collaterally attack the sentence; and

(O) that, if convicted, a defendant who is not a United States citizen may be removed from the United States, denied citizenship, and denied admission to the United States in the future.

(2) Ensuring That a Plea Is Voluntary. Before accepting a plea of guilty or nolo contendere, the court must address the defendant personally in open court and determine that the plea is voluntary and did not result from force, threats, or promises (other than promises in a plea agreement).

(3) Determining the Factual Basis for a Plea. Before entering judgment on a guilty plea, the court must determine that there is a factual basis for the plea.

(c) **Plea Agreement Procedure.**

(1) In General. An attorney for the government and the defendant's attorney, or the defendant when proceeding pro se, may discuss and reach a plea agreement. The court must not participate in these discussions. If the defendant pleads guilty or nolo contendere to either a charged offense or a lesser or related offense, the plea agreement may specify that an attorney for the government will:

(A) not bring, or will move to dismiss, other charges;

(B) recommend, or agree not to oppose the defendant's request, that a particular sentence or sentencing range is appropriate or that a particular provision of the Sentencing Guidelines, or policy statement, or sentencing factor does or does not apply (such a recommendation or request does not bind the court); or

(C) agree that a specific sentence or sentencing range is the appropriate disposition of the case, or that a particular provision of the Sentencing Guidelines, policy statement, or sentencing factor does or does not apply (such a recommendation or request binds the court once the court accepts the plea agreement).

(2) Disclosing a Plea Agreement. The parties must disclose the plea agreement in open court when the plea is offered, unless the court for good cause allows the parties to disclose the plea agreement in camera.

(3) Judicial Consideration of a Plea Agreement.

(A) To the extent the plea agreement is of the type specified in Rule 11(c)(1)(A) or (C), the court may accept the agreement, reject it, or defer a decision until the court has reviewed the presentence report.

(B) To the extent the plea agreement is of the type specified in Rule 11(c)(l)(B), the court must advise the defendant that the defendant has no right to withdraw the plea if the court does not follow the recommendation or request.

(4) Accepting a Plea Agreement. If the court accepts the plea agreement, it must inform the defendant that to the extent the plea agreement is of the type specified in Rule 11(c)(1)(A) or (C), the agreed disposition will be included in the judgment.

(5) Rejecting a Plea Agreement. If the court rejects a plea agreement containing provisions of the type specified in Rule 11(c)(1)(A) or (C), the court must do the following on the record and in open court (or, for good cause, in camera):

(A) inform the parties that the court rejects the plea agreement;

(B) advise the defendant personally that the court is not required to follow the plea agreement and give the defendant an opportunity to withdraw the plea; and

(C) advise the defendant personally that if the plea is not withdrawn, the court may dispose of the case less favorably toward the defendant than the plea agreement contemplated.

(d) Withdrawing a Guilty or Nolo Contendere Plea. A defendant may withdraw a plea of guilty or nolo contendere:

(1) before the court accepts the plea, for any reason or no reason; or

(2) after the court accepts the plea but before it imposes sentence if:

(A) the court rejects a plea agreement under Rule 11(c)(5); or

(B) the defendant can show a fair and just reason for requesting the withdrawal.

(e) Finality of a Guilty or Nolo Contendere Plea. After the court imposes sentence, the defendant may not withdraw a plea of guilty or nolo contendere, and the plea may be set aside only on direct appeal or collateral attack.

(f) Admissibility or Inadmissibility of a Plea, Plea Discussions, and Related Statements. The admissibility or inadmissibility of a plea, a plea discussion, and any related statement is governed by Federal Rule of Evidence 410.

(g) Recording the Proceedings. The proceedings during which the defendant enters a plea must be recorded by a court reporter or by a suitable recording device. If there is a guilty plea or a nolo contendere plea, the record must include the inquiries and advice to the defendant required under Rule 11(b) and (c).

(h) Harmless Error. A variance from the requirements of this rule is harmless error if it does not affect substantial rights.

Rule 12.1. Notice of an Alibi Defense

(a) Government's Request for Notice and Defendant's Response.

(1) Government's Request. An attorney for the government may request in writing that the defendant notify an attorney for the government of any intended alibi defense. The request must state the time, date, and place of the alleged offense.

(2) Defendant's Response. Within 14 days after the request, or at some other time the court sets, the defendant must serve written notice on an attorney for the government of any intended alibi defense. The defendant's notice must state:

(A) each specific place where the defendant claims to have been at the time of the alleged offense; and

(B) the name, address, and telephone number of each alibi witness on whom the defendant intends to rely.

(b) Disclosing Government Witnesses.

(1) Disclosure.

(A) In general. If the defendant serves a Rule 12.1(a)(2) notice, an attorney for the government must disclose in writing to the defendant or the defendant's attorney:

(i) the name, address, and telephone number of each witness the government intends to rely on to establish the defendant's presence at the scene of the alleged offense; and

(ii) each government rebuttal witness to the defendant's alibi defense.

(B) Victim's Address and Telephone Number. If the government intends to rely on a victim's testimony to establish that the defendant was present at the scene of the alleged offense and the defendant establishes a need for the victim's address and telephone number, the court may:

(i) order the government to provide the information in writing to the defendant or the defendant's attorney; or

(ii) fashion a reasonable procedure that allows preparation of the defense and also protects the victim's interests.

(2) Time to Disclose. Unless the court directs otherwise, an attorney for the government must give its Rule 12.1(b)(1) disclosure within 14 days after the defendant serves notice of an intended alibi defense under Rule 12.1(a)(2), but no later than 14 days before trial.

(c) **Continuing Duty to Disclose.**

(1) In General. Both an attorney for the government and the defendant must promptly disclose in writing to the other party the name of each additional witness—and the address and telephone number of each additional witness other than a victim—if:

(A) the disclosing party learns of the witness before or during trial; and

(B) the witness should have been disclosed under Rule 12.1(a) or (b) if the disclosing party had known of the witness earlier.

(2) Address and Telephone Number of an Additional Victim Witness. The address and telephone number of an additional victim witness must not be disclosed except as provided in Rule 12.1(b)(1)(B).

(d) **Exceptions.** For good cause, the court may grant an exception to any requirement of Rule 12.1(a)-(c).

(e) **Failure to Comply.** If a party fails to comply with this rule, the court may exclude the testimony of any undisclosed witness regarding the defendant's alibi. This rule does not limit the defendant's right to testify.

(f) **Inadmissibility of Withdrawn Intention.** Evidence of an intention to rely on an alibi defense, later withdrawn, or of a statement made in connection with that intention, is not, in any civil or criminal proceeding, admissible against the person who gave notice of the intention.

Rule 13. Joint Trial of Separate Cases

The court may order that separate cases be tried together as though brought in a single indictment or information if all offenses and all defendants could have been joined in a single indictment or information.

Rule 14. Relief from Prejudicial Joinder

(a) **Relief.** If the joinder of offenses or defendants in an indictment, an information, or a consolidation for trial appears to prejudice a defendant or the government, the court may order separate trials of counts, sever the defendants' trials, or provide any other relief that justice requires.

(b) Defendant's Statements. Before ruling on a defendant's motion to sever, the court may order an attorney for the government to deliver to the court for in camera inspection any defendant's statement that the government intends to use as evidence.

Rule 16.   Discovery and Inspection

(a) Government's Disclosure.

(1) Information Subject to Disclosure.

(A) Defendant's Oral Statement. Upon a defendant's request, the government must disclose to the defendant the substance of any relevant oral statement made by the defendant, before or after arrest, in response to interrogation by a person the defendant knew was a government agent if the government intends to use the statement at trial.

(B) Defendant's Written or Recorded Statement. Upon a defendant's request, the government must disclose to the defendant, and make available for inspection, copying, or photographing, all of the following:

(i) any relevant written or recorded statement by the defendant if:

- the statement is within the government's possession, custody, or control; and
- the attorney for the government knows—or through due diligence could know—that the statement exists;

(ii) the portion of any written record containing the substance of any relevant oral statement made before or after arrest if the defendant made the statement in response to interrogation by a person the defendant knew was a government agent; and

(iii) the defendant's recorded testimony before a grand jury relating to the charged offense.

(C) Organizational Defendant. Upon a defendant's request, if the defendant is an organization, the government must disclose to the defendant any statement described in Rule 16(a)(1)(A) and (B) if the government contends that the person making the statement:

(i) was legally able to bind the defendant regarding the subject of the statement because of that person's position as the defendant's director, officer, employee, or agent; or

(ii) was personally involved in the alleged conduct constituting the offense and was legally able to bind the defendant regarding that conduct because of that person's position as the defendant's director, officer, employee, or agent.

(D) Defendant's Prior Record. Upon a defendant's request, the government must furnish the defendant with a copy of the defendant's prior criminal record that is within the government's possession, custody, or control if the attorney for the government knows—or through due diligence could know—that the record exists.

(E) Documents and Objects. Upon a defendant's request, the government must permit the defendant to inspect and to copy or photograph books, papers, documents, data, photographs, tangible objects, buildings or places, or copies or portions of any of these items, if the item is within the government's possession, custody, or control and:

(i) the item is material to preparing the defense;

(ii) the government intends to use the item in its case-in-chief at trial; or

(iii) the item was obtained from or belongs to the defendant.

(F) Reports of Examinations and Tests. Upon a defendant's request, the government must permit a defendant to inspect and to copy or photograph the results or reports of any physical or mental examination and of any scientific test or experiment if:

(i) the item is within the government's possession, custody, or control;

(ii) the attorney for the government knows—or through due diligence could know—that the item exists; and

(iii) the item is material to preparing the defense or the government intends to use the item in its case-in-chief at trial.

(G) Expert Witnesses. At the defendant's request, the government must give to the defendant a written summary of any testimony that the government intends to use under Rules 702, 703, or 705 of the Federal Rules of Evidence during its case-in-chief at trial. If the government requests discovery under subdivision (b)(1)(C)(ii) and the defendant complies, the government must, at the defendant's request, give to the defendant a written summary of testimony that the government intends to use under Rules 702, 703, or 705 of the Federal Rules of Evidence as evidence at trial on the issue of the defendant's mental condition. The summary provided under this subparagraph must describe the witness's opinions, the bases and reasons for those opinions, and the witness's qualifications.

(2) Information Not Subject to Disclosure. Except as permitted by Rule 16(a)(1)(A)-(D), (F), and (G), this rule does not authorize the discovery or inspection of reports, memoranda, or other internal government documents made by an attorney for the government or other government agent in connection with investigating or prosecuting the case. Nor does this rule authorize the discovery or inspection of statements made by prospective government witnesses except as provided in 18 U.S.C. §3500.

(3) Grand Jury Transcripts. This rule does not apply to the discovery or inspection of a grand jury's recorded proceedings, except as provided in Rules 6, 12(h), 16(a)(1), and 26.2.

(b) Defendant's Disclosure.

(1) Information Subject to Disclosure.

(A) Documents and Objects. If a defendant requests disclosure under Rule 16(a)(1)(E) and the government complies, then the defendant must permit the government, upon request, to inspect and to copy or photograph books, papers, documents, data, photographs, tangible objects, buildings or places, or copies or portions of any of these items if:

(i) the item is within the defendant's possession, custody, or control; and

(ii) the defendant intends to use the item in the defendant's case-in-chief at trial.

(B) Reports of Examinations and Tests. If a defendant requests disclosure under Rule 16(a)(1)(F) and the government complies, the defendant must permit the government, upon request, to inspect and to copy or photograph the results or reports of any physical or mental examination and of any scientific test or experiment if:

(i) the item is within the defendant's possession, custody, or control; and

(ii) the defendant intends to use the item in the defendant's case-in-chief at trial, or intends to call the witness who prepared the report and the report relates to the witness's testimony.

(C) Expert Witnesses. The defendant must, at the government's request, give to the government a written summary of any testimony that the defendant intends to use under Rules 702, 703, or 705 of the Federal Rules of Evidence as evidence at trial, if—

(i) the defendant requests disclosure under subdivision (a)(1)(G) and the government complies; or

(ii) the defendant has given notice under Rule 12.2(b) of an intent to present expert testimony on the defendant's mental condition.

This summary must describe the witness's opinions, the bases and reasons for those opinions, and the witness's qualifications.

(2) Information Not Subject to Disclosure. Except for scientific or medical reports, Rule 16(b)(1) does not authorize discovery or inspection of:

(A) reports, memoranda, or other documents made by the defendant, or the defendant's attorney or agent, during the case's investigation or defense; or

(B) a statement made to the defendant, or the defendant's attorney or agent, by:

(i) the defendant;

(ii) a government or defense witness; or

(iii) a prospective government or defense witness.

(c) Continuing Duty to Disclose. A party who discovers additional evidence or material before or during trial must promptly disclose its existence to the other party or the court if:

(1) the evidence or material is subject to discovery or inspection under this rule; and

(2) the other party previously requested, or the court ordered, its production.

(d) Regulating Discovery.

(1) Protective and Modifying Orders. At any time the court may, for good cause, deny, restrict, or defer discovery or inspection, or grant other appropriate relief. The court may permit a party to show good cause by a written statement that the court will inspect ex parte. If relief is granted, the court must preserve the entire text of the party's statement under seal.

(2) Failure to Comply. If a party fails to comply with this rule, the court may:

(A) order that party to permit the discovery or inspection; specify its time, place, and manner; and prescribe other just terms and conditions;

(B) grant a continuance;

(C) prohibit that party from introducing the undisclosed evidence; or

(D) enter any other order that is just under the circumstances.

Rule 16.1.   Pretrial Discovery Conference; Request for Court Action

(a) Discovery Conference. No later than 14 days after the arraignment, the attorney for the government and the defendant's attorney must confer and try to agree on a timetable and procedures for pretrial disclosure under Rule 16.

(b) Request for Court Action. After the discovery conference, one or both parties may ask the court to determine or modify the time, place, manner, or other aspects of disclosure to facilitate preparation for trial.

Rule 17.   Subpoena

(a) Content. A subpoena must state the court's name and the title of the proceeding, include the seal of the court, and command the witness to attend and testify at the time and place the subpoena specifies. The clerk must issue a blank subpoena—signed and sealed—to the party requesting it, and that party must fill in the blanks before the subpoena is served.

(b) Defendant Unable to Pay. Upon a defendant's ex parte application, the court must order that a subpoena be issued for a named witness if the defendant shows an inability to pay the witness's fees and the necessity of the witness's presence for an adequate defense. If the court orders a subpoena to be issued, the process costs and witness fees will be paid in the same manner as those paid for witnesses the government subpoenas.

(c) Producing Documents and Objects.

(1) In General. A subpoena may order the witness to produce any books, papers, documents, data, or other objects the subpoena

designates. The court may direct the witness to produce the designated items in court before trial or before they are to be offered in evidence. When the items arrive, the court may permit the parties and their attorneys to inspect all or part of them.

(2) Quashing or Modifying the Subpoena. On motion made promptly, the court may quash or modify the subpoena if compliance would be unreasonable or oppressive.

(3) Subpoena for Personal or Confidential Information About a Victim. After a complaint, indictment, or information is filed, a subpoena requiring the production of personal or confidential information about a victim may be served on a third party only by court order. Before entering the order and unless there are exceptional circumstances, the court must require giving notice to the victim so that the victim can move to quash or modify the subpoena or otherwise object.

(d) Service. A marshal, a deputy marshal, or any nonparty who is at least 18 years old may serve a subpoena. The server must deliver a copy of the subpoena to the witness and must tender to the witness one day's witness-attendance fee and the legal mileage allowance. The server need not tender the attendance fee or mileage allowance when the United States, a federal officer, or a federal agency has requested the subpoena.

(e) Place of Service.

(1) In the United States. A subpoena requiring a witness to attend a hearing or trial may be served at any place within the United States.

(2) In a Foreign Country. If the witness is in a foreign country, 28 U.S.C. §1783 governs the subpoena's service.

(f) Issuing a Deposition Subpoena.

(1) Issuance. A court order to take a deposition authorizes the clerk in the district where the deposition is to be taken to issue a subpoena for any witness named or described in the order.

(2) Place. After considering the convenience of the witness and the parties, the court may order—and the subpoena may require—the witness to appear anywhere the court designates.

(g) Contempt. The court (other than a magistrate judge) may hold in contempt a witness who, without adequate excuse, disobeys a subpoena issued by a federal court in that district. A magistrate judge may hold in contempt a witness who, without adequate excuse, disobeys a subpoena issued by that magistrate judge as provided in 28 U.S.C. §636(e).

(h) Information Not Subject to a Subpoena. No party may subpoena a statement of a witness or of a prospective witness under this rule. Rule 26.2 governs the production of the statement.

Rule 18. Place of Prosecution and Trial

Unless a statute or these rules permit otherwise, the government must prosecute an offense in a district where the offense was committed. The court must set the place of trial within the district with due regard for the convenience of the defendant, any victim, and the witnesses, and the prompt administration of justice.

Rule 21. Transfer for Trial

(a) **For Prejudice.** Upon the defendant's motion, the court must transfer the proceeding against that defendant to another district if the court is satisfied that so great a prejudice against the defendant exists in the transferring district that the defendant cannot obtain a fair and impartial trial there.

(b) **For Convenience.** Upon the defendant's motion, the court may transfer the proceeding, or one or more counts, against that defendant to another district for the convenience of the parties, any victim, and the witnesses, and in the interest of justice.

(c) **Proceedings on Transfer.** When the court orders a transfer, the clerk must send to the transferee district the file, or a certified copy, and any bail taken. The prosecution will then continue in the transferee district.

(d) **Time to File a Motion to Transfer.** A motion to transfer may be made at or before arraignment or at any other time the court or these rules prescribe.

Rule 23. Jury or Nonjury Trial

(a) **Jury Trial.** If the defendant is entitled to a jury trial, the trial must be by jury unless:

   (1) the defendant waives a jury trial in writing;
   (2) the government consents; and

(3) the court approves.

(b) Jury Size.

(1) In General. A jury consists of 12 persons unless this rule provides otherwise.

(2) Stipulation for a Smaller Jury. At any time before the verdict, the parties may, with the court's approval, stipulate in writing that:

(A) the jury may consist of fewer than 12 persons; or

(B) a jury of fewer than 12 persons may return a verdict if the court finds it necessary to excuse a juror for good cause after the trial begins.

(3) Court Order for a Jury of 11. After the jury has retired to deliberate, the court may permit a jury of 11 persons to return a verdict, even without a stipulation by the parties, if the court finds good cause to excuse a juror.

(c) Nonjury Trial. In a case tried without a jury, the court must find the defendant guilty or not guilty. If a party requests before the finding of guilty or not guilty, the court must state its specific findings of fact in open court or in a written decision or opinion.

Rule 24.   Trial Jurors

(a) Examination.

(1) In General. The court may examine prospective jurors or may permit the attorneys for the parties to do so.

(2) Court Examination. If the court examines the jurors, it must permit the attorneys for the parties to:

(A) ask further questions that the court considers proper; or

(B) submit further questions that the court may ask if it considers them proper.

(b) Peremptory Challenges. Each side is entitled to the number of peremptory challenges to prospective jurors specified below. The court may allow additional peremptory challenges to multiple defendants, and may allow the defendants to exercise those challenges separately or jointly.

(1) Capital Case. Each side has 20 peremptory challenges when the government seeks the death penalty.

(2) Other Felony Case. The government has 6 peremptory challenges and the defendant or defendants jointly have 10 peremptory challenges when the defendant is charged with a crime punishable by imprisonment of more than one year.

(3) Misdemeanor Case. Each side has 3 peremptory challenges when the defendant is charged with a crime punishable by fine, imprisonment of one year or less, or both.

(c) Alternate Jurors.

(1) In General. The court may impanel up to 6 alternate jurors to replace any jurors who are unable to perform or who are disqualified from performing their duties.

(2) Procedure.

(A) Alternate jurors must have the same qualifications and be selected and sworn in the same manner as any other juror.

(B) Alternate jurors replace jurors in the same sequence in which the alternates were selected. An alternate juror who replaces a juror has the same authority as the other jurors.

(3) Retaining Alternate Jurors. The court may retain alternate jurors after the jury retires to deliberate. The court must ensure that a retained alternate does not discuss the case with anyone until that alternate replaces a juror or is discharged. If an alternate replaces a juror after deliberations have begun, the court must instruct the jury to begin its deliberations anew.

(4) Peremptory Challenges. Each side is entitled to the number of additional peremptory challenges to prospective alternate jurors specified below. These additional challenges may be used only to remove alternate jurors.

(A) One or Two Alternates. One additional peremptory challenge is permitted when one or two alternates are impaneled.

(B) Three or Four Alternates. Two additional peremptory challenges are permitted when three or four alternates are impaneled.

(C) Five or Six Alternates. Three additional peremptory challenges are permitted when five or six alternates are impaneled.

Rule 26.2. Producing a Witness's Statement

(a) Motion to Produce. After a witness other than the defendant has testified on direct examination, the court, on motion of a party who did not call the witness, must order an attorney for the government or the defendant and the defendant's attorney to produce, for the examination and use of the moving party, any statement of the witness that is in their possession and that relates to the subject matter of the witness's testimony.

(b) Producing the Entire Statement. If the entire statement relates to the subject matter of the witness's testimony, the court must order that the statement be delivered to the moving party.

(c) Producing a Redacted Statement. If the party who called the witness claims that the statement contains information that is privileged or does not relate to the subject matter of the witness's testimony, the court must inspect the statement in camera. After excising any privileged or unrelated portions, the court must order delivery of the redacted statement to the moving party. If the defendant objects to an excision, the court must preserve the entire statement with the excised portion indicated, under seal, as part of the record.

(d) Recess to Examine a Statement. The court may recess the proceedings to allow time for a party to examine the statement and prepare for its use.

(e) Sanction for Failure to Produce or Deliver a Statement. If the party who called the witness disobeys an order to produce or deliver a statement, the court must strike the witness's testimony from the record. If an attorney for the government disobeys the order, the court must declare a mistrial if justice so requires.

(f) "Statement" Defined. As used in this rule, a witness's "statement" means:

(1) a written statement that the witness makes and signs, or otherwise adopts or approves;

(2) a substantially verbatim, contemporaneously recorded recital of the witness's oral statement that is contained in any recording or any transcription of a recording; or

(3) the witness's statement to a grand jury, however taken or recorded, or a transcription of such a statement.

(g) Scope. This rule applies at trial, at a suppression hearing under Rule 12, and to the extent specified in the following rules:

(1) Rule 5.1(h) (preliminary hearing);

(2) Rule 32(i)(2) (sentencing);

(3) Rule 32.1(e) (hearing to revoke or modify probation or supervised release);

(4) Rule 46(j) (detention hearing); and

(5) Rule 8 of the Rules Governing Proceedings under 28 U.S.C. §2255.

Rule 26.3. Mistrial

Before ordering a mistrial, the court must give each defendant and the government an opportunity to comment on the propriety of the order, to state whether that party consents or objects, and to suggest alternatives.

Rule 29. Motion for a Judgment of Acquittal

(a) **Before Submission to the Jury.** After the government closes its evidence or after the close of all the evidence, the court on the defendant's motion must enter a judgment of acquittal of any offense for which the evidence is insufficient to sustain a conviction. The court may on its own consider whether the evidence is insufficient to sustain a conviction. If the court denies a motion for a judgment of acquittal at the close of the government's evidence, the defendant may offer evidence without having reserved the right to do so.

(b) **Reserving Decision.** The court may reserve decision on the motion, proceed with the trial (where the motion is made before the close of all the evidence), submit the case to the jury, and decide the motion either before the jury returns a verdict or after it returns a verdict of guilty or is discharged without having returned a verdict. If the court reserves decision, it must decide the motion on the basis of the evidence at the time the ruling was reserved.

(c) **After Jury Verdict or Discharge.**

(1) Time for a Motion. A defendant may move for a judgment of acquittal, or renew such a motion, within 14 days after a guilty verdict or after the court discharges the jury, whichever is later.

(2) Ruling on the Motion. If the jury has returned a guilty verdict, the court may set aside the verdict and enter an acquittal. If the jury has failed to return a verdict, the court may enter a judgment of acquittal.

(3) No Prior Motion Required. A defendant is not required to move for a judgment of acquittal before the court submits the case to the jury as a prerequisite for making such a motion after jury discharge.

(d) **Conditional Ruling on a Motion for a New Trial.**

(1) Motion for a New Trial. If the court enters a judgment of acquittal after a guilty verdict, the court must also conditionally determine whether any motion for a new trial should be granted if

the judgment of acquittal is later vacated or reversed. The court must specify the reasons for that determination.

(2) Finality. The court's order conditionally granting a motion for a new trial does not affect the finality of the judgment of acquittal.

(3) Appeal.

(A) Grant of a Motion for a New Trial. If the court conditionally grants a motion for a new trial and an appellate court later reverses the judgment of acquittal, the trial court must proceed with the new trial unless the appellate court orders otherwise.

(B) Denial of a Motion for a New Trial. If the court conditionally denies a motion for a new trial, an appellee may assert that the denial was erroneous. If the appellate court later reverses the judgment of acquittal, the trial court must proceed as the appellate court directs.

Rule 29.1. Closing Argument

Closing arguments proceed in the following order:
(a) the government argues;
(b) the defense argues; and
(c) the government rebuts.

Rule 30. Jury Instructions

(a) In General. Any party may request in writing that the court instruct the jury on the law as specified in the request. The request must be made at the close of the evidence or at any earlier time that the court reasonably sets. When the request is made, the requesting party must furnish a copy to every other party.

(b) Ruling on a Request. The court must inform the parties before closing arguments how it intends to rule on the requested instructions.

(c) Time for Giving Instructions. The court may instruct the jury before or after the arguments are completed, or at both times.

(d) Objections to Instructions. A party who objects to any portion of the instructions or to a failure to give a requested instruction must inform the court of the specific objection and the grounds for the objection before the jury retires to deliberate. An opportunity must be given to object out of the jury's hearing and, on request, out of the jury's presence. Failure to object in accordance with this rule precludes appellate review, except as permitted under Rule 52(b).

Rule 31. Jury Verdict

(a) **Return.** The jury must return its verdict to a judge in open court. The verdict must be unanimous.

(b) **Partial Verdicts, Mistrial, and Retrial.**

(1) Multiple Defendants. If there are multiple defendants, the jury may return a verdict at any time during its deliberations as to any defendant about whom it has agreed.

(2) Multiple Counts. If the jury cannot agree on all counts as to any defendant, the jury may return a verdict on those counts on which it has agreed.

(3) Mistrial and Retrial. If the jury cannot agree on a verdict on one or more counts, the court may declare a mistrial on those counts. The government may retry any defendant on any count on which the jury could not agree.

(c) **Lesser Offense or Attempt.** A defendant may be found guilty of any of the following:

(1) an offense necessarily included in the offense charged;

(2) an attempt to commit the offense charged; or

(3) an attempt to commit an offense necessarily included in the offense charged, if the attempt is an offense in its own right.

(d) **Jury Poll.** After a verdict is returned but before the jury is discharged, the court must on a party's request, or may on its own, poll the jurors individually. If the poll reveals a lack of unanimity, the court may direct the jury to deliberate further or may declare a mistrial and discharge the jury.

Rule 32. Sentencing and Judgment

(a) **[Reserved.]**

(b) **Time of Sentencing.**

(1) In General. The court must impose sentence without unnecessary delay.

(2) Changing Time Limits. The court may, for good cause, change any time limits prescribed in this rule.

(c) Presentence Investigation.

(1) Required Investigation.

(A) In General. The probation officer must conduct a presentence investigation and submit a report to the court before it imposes sentence unless:

(i) 18 U.S.C. §3593(c) or another statute requires otherwise; or

(ii) the court finds that the information in the record enables it to meaningfully exercise its sentencing authority under 18 U.S.C. §3553, and the court explains its finding on the record.

(B) Restitution. If the law permits restitution, the probation officer must conduct an investigation and submit a report that contains sufficient information for the court to order restitution.

(2) Interviewing the Defendant. The probation officer who interviews a defendant as part of a presentence investigation must, on request, give the defendant's attorney notice and a reasonable opportunity to attend the interview.

(d) Presentence Report.

(1) Applying the Advisory Sentencing Guidelines. The presentence report must:

(A) identify all applicable guidelines and policy statements of the Sentencing Commission;

(B) calculate the defendant's offense level and criminal history category;

(C) state the resulting sentencing range and kinds of sentences available;

(D) identify any factor relevant to:

(i) the appropriate kind of sentence, or

(ii) the appropriate sentence within the applicable sentencing range; and

(E) identify any basis for departing from the applicable sentencing range.

(2) Additional Information. The presentence report must also contain the following:

(A) the defendant's history and characteristics, including:

(i) any prior criminal record;

(ii) the defendant's financial condition; and

(iii) any circumstances affecting the defendant's behavior that may be helpful in imposing sentence or in correctional treatment;

(B) information that assesses any financial, social, psychological, and medical impact on any victim;

(C) when appropriate, the nature and extent of nonprison programs and resources available to the defendant;

(D) when the law provides for restitution, information sufficient for a restitution order;

(E) if the court orders a study under 18 U.S.C. §3552(b), any resulting report and recommendation;

(F) a statement of whether the government seeks forfeiture under Rule 32.2 and any other law; and

(G) any other information that the court requires, including information relevant to the factors under 18 U.S.C. §3553(a).

(3) Exclusions. The presentence report must exclude the following:

(A) any diagnoses that, if disclosed, might seriously disrupt a rehabilitation program;

(B) any sources of information obtained upon a promise of confidentiality; and

(C) any other information that, if disclosed, might result in physical or other harm to the defendant or others.

(e) Disclosing the Report and Recommendation.

(1) Time to Disclose. Unless the defendant has consented in writing, the probation officer must not submit a presentence report to the court or disclose its contents to anyone until the defendant has pleaded guilty or nolo contendere, or has been found guilty.

(2) Minimum Required Notice. The probation officer must give the presentence report to the defendant, the defendant's attorney, and an attorney for the government at least 35 days before sentencing unless the defendant waives this minimum period.

(3) Sentence Recommendation. By local rule or by order in a case, the court may direct the probation officer not to disclose to anyone other than the court the officer's recommendation on the sentence.

(f) Objecting to the Report.

(1) Time to Object. Within 14 days after receiving the presentence report, the parties must state in writing any objections, including objections to material information, sentencing guideline ranges, and policy statements contained in or omitted from the report.

(2) Serving Objections. An objecting party must provide a copy of its objections to the opposing party and to the probation officer.

(3) Action on Objections. After receiving objections, the probation officer may meet with the parties to discuss the objections. The probation officer may then investigate further and revise the presentence report as appropriate.

(g) Submitting the Report. At least 14 days before sentencing, the probation officer must submit to the court and to the parties the presentence report and an addendum containing any unresolved objections, the grounds for those objections, and the probation officer's comments on them.

(h) Notice of Possible Departure from Sentencing Guidelines. Before the court may depart from the applicable sentencing range on a ground not identified for departure either in the presentence report or in a party's prehearing submission, the court must give the parties reasonable notice that it is contemplating such a departure. The notice must specify any ground on which the court is contemplating a departure.

(i) Sentencing.

(1) In General. At sentencing, the court:

(A) must verify that the defendant and the defendant's attorney have read and discussed the presentence report and any addendum to the report;

(B) must give to the defendant and an attorney for the government a written summary of—or summarize in camera—any information excluded from the presentence report under Rule 32(d)(3) on which the court will rely in sentencing, and give them a reasonable opportunity to comment on that information;

(C) must allow the parties' attorneys to comment on the probation officer's determinations and other matters relating to an appropriate sentence; and

(D) may, for good cause, allow a party to make a new objection at any time before sentence is imposed.

(2) Introducing Evidence; Producing a Statement. The court may permit the parties to introduce evidence on the objections. If a witness testifies at sentencing, Rule 26.2(a)-(d) and (f) applies. If a party fails to comply with a Rule 26.2 order to produce a witness's statement, the court must not consider that witness's testimony.

(3) Court Determinations. At sentencing, the court:

(A) may accept any undisputed portion of the presentence report as a finding of fact;

(B) must—for any disputed portion of the presentence report or other controverted matter—rule on the dispute or determine that a ruling is unnecessary either because the matter will not affect sentencing, or because the court will not consider the matter in sentencing; and

(C) must append a copy of the court's determinations under this rule to any copy of the presentence report made available to the Bureau of Prisons.

(4) Opportunity to Speak.

(A) By a Party. Before imposing sentence, the court must:

(i) provide the defendant's attorney an opportunity to speak on the defendant's behalf;

(ii) address the defendant personally in order to permit the defendant to speak or present any information to mitigate the sentence; and

(iii) provide an attorney for the government an opportunity to speak equivalent to that of the defendant's attorney.

(B) By a Victim. Before imposing sentence, the court must address any victim of the crime who is present at sentencing and must permit the victim to be reasonably heard.

(C) By a Victim of a Felony Offense. Before imposing sentence, the court must address any victim of a felony offense, not involving violence or sexual abuse, who is present at sentencing and must permit the victim to speak or submit any information about the sentence. If the felony offense involved multiple victims, the court may limit the number of victims who will address the court.

(D) In Camera Proceedings. Upon a party's motion and for good cause, the court may hear in camera any statement made under Rule 32(i)(4).

(j) Defendant's Right to Appeal.

(1) Advice of a Right to Appeal.

(A) Appealing a Conviction. If the defendant pleaded not guilty and was convicted, after sentencing the court must advise the defendant of the right to appeal the conviction.

(B) Appealing a Sentence. After sentencing—regardless of the defendant's plea—the court must advise the defendant of any right to appeal the sentence.

(C) Appeal Costs. The court must advise a defendant who is unable to pay appeal costs of the right to ask for permission to appeal in forma pauperis.

(2) Clerk's Filing of Notice. If the defendant so requests, the clerk must immediately prepare and file a notice of appeal on the defendant's behalf.

(k) Judgment.

(1) In General. In the judgment of conviction, the court must set forth the plea, the jury verdict or the court's findings, the adjudication, and the sentence. If the defendant is found not guilty or is otherwise entitled to be discharged, the court must so order. The judge must sign the judgment, and the clerk must enter it.

(2) Criminal Forfeiture. Forfeiture procedures are governed by Rule 32.2.

Rule 33. New Trial

(a) Defendant's Motion. Upon the defendant's motion, the court may vacate any judgment and grant a new trial if the interest of justice so requires. If the case was tried without a jury, the court may take additional testimony and enter a new judgment.

(b) Time to File.

(1) Newly Discovered Evidence. Any motion for a new trial grounded on newly discovered evidence must be filed within 3 years after the verdict or finding of guilty. If an appeal is pending, the court may not grant a motion for a new trial until the appellate court remands the case.

(2) Other Grounds. Any motion for a new trial grounded on any reason other than newly discovered evidence must be filed within 14 days after the verdict or finding of guilty.

Rule 41. Search and Seizure

(a) Scope and Definitions.

(1) Scope. This rule does not modify any statute regulating search or seizure, or the issuance and execution of a search warrant in special circumstances.

(2) Definitions. The following definitions apply under this rule:

(A) "Property" includes documents, books, papers, any other tangible objects, and information.

(B) "Daytime" means the hours between 6:00 a.m. and 10:00 p.m. according to local time.

(C) "Federal law enforcement officer" means a government agent (other than an attorney for the government) who is engaged in enforcing the criminal laws and is within any category of officers authorized by the Attorney General to request a search warrant.

    (D) "Domestic terrorism" and "international terrorism" have the meanings set out in 18 U.S.C. §2331.

    (E) "Tracking device" has the meaning set out in 18 U.S.C. §3117(b).

(b) Venue for a Warrant Application. At the request of a federal law enforcement officer or an attorney for the government:

    (1) a magistrate judge with authority in the district—or if none is reasonably available, a judge of a state court of record in the district—has authority to issue a warrant to search for and seize a person or property located within the district;

    (2) a magistrate judge with authority in the district has authority to issue a warrant for a person or property outside the district if the person or property is located within the district when the warrant is issued but might move or be moved outside the district before the warrant is executed;

    (3) a magistrate judge—in an investigation of domestic terrorism or international terrorism—with authority in any district in which activities related to the terrorism may have occurred has authority to issue a warrant for a person or property within or outside that district;

    (4) a magistrate judge with authority in the district has authority to issue a warrant to install within the district a tracking device; the warrant may authorize use of the device to track the movement of a person or property located within the district, outside the district, or both; and

    (5) a magistrate judge having authority in any district where activities related to the crime may have occurred, or in the District of Columbia, may issue a warrant for property that is located outside the jurisdiction of any state or district, but within any of the following:

    (A) a United States territory, possession, or commonwealth;

    (B) the premises—no matter who owns them—of a United States diplomatic or consular mission in a foreign state, including any appurtenant building, part of a building, or land used for the mission's purposes; or

    (C) a residence and any appurtenant land owned or leased by the United States and used by United States personnel assigned to a United States diplomatic or consular mission in a foreign state.

    (6) a magistrate judge with authority in any district where activities related to a crime may have occurred has authority to issue a

warrant to use remote access to search electronic storage media and to seize or copy electronically stored information located within or outside that district if:

(A) the district where the media or information is located has been concealed through technological means; or

(B) in an investigation of a violation of 18 U.S.C. § 1030(a)(5), the media are protected computers that have been damaged without authorization and are located in five or more districts.

(c) Persons or Property Subject to Search or Seizure. A warrant may be issued for any of the following:

(1) evidence of a crime;

(2) contraband, fruits of crime, or other items illegally possessed;

(3) property designed for use, intended for use, or used in committing a crime; or

(4) a person to be arrested or a person who is unlawfully restrained.

(d) Obtaining a Warrant.

(1) In General. After receiving an affidavit or other information, a magistrate judge—or if authorized by Rule 41(b), a judge of a state court of record—must issue the warrant if there is probable cause to search for and seize a person or property or to install and use a tracking device.

(2) Requesting a Warrant in the Presence of a Judge.

(A) Warrant on an Affidavit. When a federal law enforcement officer or an attorney for the government presents an affidavit in support of a warrant, the judge may require the affiant to appear personally and may examine under oath the affiant and any witness the affiant produces.

(B) Warrant on Sworn Testimony. The judge may wholly or partially dispense with a written affidavit and base a warrant on sworn testimony if doing so is reasonable under the circumstances.

(C) Recording Testimony. Testimony taken in support of a warrant must be recorded by a court reporter or by a suitable recording device, and the judge must file the transcript or recording with the clerk, along with any affidavit.

(3) Requesting a Warrant by Telephonic or Other Reliable Electronic Means. In accordance with Rule 4.1, a magistrate judge may issue a warrant based on information communicated by telephone or other reliable electronic means.

(e) Issuing the Warrant.

(1) In General. The magistrate judge or a judge of a state court of record must issue the warrant to an officer authorized to execute it.

(2) Contents of the Warrant.

(A) Warrant to Search for and Seize a Person or Property. Except for a tracking-device warrant, the warrant must identify the person or property to be searched, identify any person or property to be seized, and designate the magistrate judge to whom it must be returned. The warrant must command the officer to:

(i) execute the warrant within a specified time no longer than 14 days;

(ii) execute the warrant during the daytime, unless the judge for good cause expressly authorizes execution at another time; and

(iii) return the warrant to the magistrate judge designated in the warrant.

(B) Warrant Seeking Electronically Stored Information. A warrant under Rule 41(e)(2)(A) may authorize the seizure of electronic storage media or the seizure or copying of electronically stored information. Unless otherwise specified, the warrant authorizes a later review of the media or information consistent with the warrant. The time for executing the warrant in Rule 41(e)(2)(A) and (f)(1)(A) refers to the seizure or on-site copying of the media or information, and not to any later off-site copying or review.

(C) Warrant for a Tracking Device. A tracking-device warrant must identify the person or property to be tracked, designate the magistrate judge to whom it must be returned, and specify a reasonable length of time that the device may be used. The time must not exceed 45 days from the date the warrant was issued. The court may, for good cause, grant one or more extensions for a reasonable period not to exceed 45 days each. The warrant must command the officer to:

(i) complete any installation authorized by the warrant within a specified time no longer than 10 days;

(ii) perform any installation authorized by the warrant during the daytime, unless the judge for good cause expressly authorizes installation at another time; and

(iii) return the warrant to the judge designated in the warrant.

(f) Executing and Returning the Warrant.

(1) Warrant to Search for and Seize a Person or Property.

(A) Noting the Time. The officer executing the warrant must enter on it the exact date and time it was executed.

(B) Inventory. An officer present during the execution of the warrant must prepare and verify an inventory of any property seized. The officer must do so in the presence of another officer and the person from whom, or from whose premises, the property was taken. If either one is not present, the officer must prepare and verify the inventory in the presence of at least one other credible person. In a case involving the seizure of electronic storage media or the seizure or copying of electronically stored information, the inventory may be limited to describing the physical storage media that were seized or copied. The officer may retain a copy of the electronically stored information that was seized or copied.

(C) Receipt. The officer executing the warrant must give a copy of the warrant and a receipt for the property taken to the person from whom, or from whose premises, the property was taken or leave a copy of the warrant and receipt at the place where the officer took the property. For a warrant to use remote access to search electronic storage media and seize or copy electronically stored information, the officer must make reasonable efforts to serve a copy of the warrant and receipt on the person whose property was searched or who possessed the information that was seized or copied. Service may be accomplished by any means, including electronic means, reasonably calculated to reach that person.

(D) Return. The officer executing the warrant must promptly return it—together with a copy of the inventory—to the magistrate judge designated on the warrant. The officer may do so by reliable electronic means. The judge must, on request, give a copy of the inventory to the person from whom, or from whose premises, the property was taken and to the applicant for the warrant.

(2) Warrant for a Tracking Device.

(A) Noting the Time. The officer executing a tracking-device warrant must enter on it the exact date and time the device was installed and the period during which it was used.

(B) Return. Within 10 days after the use of the tracking device has ended, the officer executing the warrant must return it to the judge designated in the warrant. The officer may do so by reliable electronic means.

(C) Service. Within 10 days after the use of the tracking device has ended, the officer executing a tracking-device warrant must serve a copy of the warrant on the person who was tracked or whose property was tracked. Service may be accomplished by delivering a copy to the person who, or whose property, was tracked; or by leaving a copy at the person's residence or usual place of abode with an individual of suitable age and discretion who resides at that location and by mailing a copy to the person's last known address. Upon request of the government, the judge may delay notice as provided in Rule 41(f)(3).

(3) Delayed Notice. Upon the government's request, a magistrate judge—or if authorized by Rule 41(b), a judge of a state court of record—may delay any notice required by this rule if the delay is authorized by statute.

(g) **Motion to Return Property.** A person aggrieved by an unlawful search and seizure of property or by the deprivation of property may move for the property's return. The motion must be filed in the district where the property was seized. The court must receive evidence on any factual issue necessary to decide the motion. If it grants the motion, the court must return the property to the movant, but may impose reasonable conditions to protect access to the property and its use in later proceedings.

(h) **Motion to Suppress.** A defendant may move to suppress evidence in the court where the trial will occur, as Rule 12 provides.

(i) **Forwarding Papers to the Clerk.** The magistrate judge to whom the warrant is returned must attach to the warrant a copy of the return, of the inventory, and of all other related papers and must deliver them to the clerk in the district where the property was seized.

Rule 43.   Defendant's Presence

(a) **When Required.** Unless this rule, Rule 5, or Rule 10 provides otherwise, the defendant must be present at:

(1) the initial appearance, the initial arraignment, and the plea;

(2) every trial stage, including jury impanelment and the return of the verdict; and

(3) sentencing.

(b) **When Not Required.** A defendant need not be present under any of the following circumstances:

(1) *Organizational Defendant.* The defendant is an organization represented by counsel who is present.

(2) *Misdemeanor Offense.* The offense is punishable by fine or by imprisonment for not more than one year, or both, and with the defendant's written consent, the court permits arraignment, plea, trial, and sentencing to occur by video teleconferencing or in the defendant's absence.

(3) *Conference or Hearing on a Legal Question.* The proceeding involves only a conference or hearing on a question of law.

(4) *Sentence Correction.* The proceeding involves the correction or reduction of sentence under Rule 35 or 18 U.S.C. § 3582(c).

(c) Waiving Continued Presence.

(1) *In General.* A defendant who was initially present at trial, or who had pleaded guilty or nolo contendere, waives the right to be present under the following circumstances:

(A) when the defendant is voluntarily absent after the trial has begun, regardless of whether the court informed the defendant of an obligation to remain during trial;

(B) in a noncapital case, when the defendant is voluntarily absent during sentencing; or

(C) when the court warns the defendant that it will remove the defendant from the courtroom for disruptive behavior, but the defendant persists in conduct that justifies removal from the courtroom.

(2) *Waiver's Effect.* If the defendant waives the right to be present, the trial may proceed to completion, including the verdict's return and sentencing, during the defendant's absence.

Rule 44.   Right to and Appointment of Counsel

(a) Right to Appointed Counsel. A defendant who is unable to obtain counsel is entitled to have counsel appointed to represent the defendant at every stage of the proceeding from initial appearance through appeal, unless the defendant waives this right.

(b) Appointment Procedure. Federal law and local court rules govern the procedure for implementing the right to counsel.

(c) Inquiry into Joint Representation.

(1) Joint Representation. Joint representation occurs when:

(A) two or more defendants have been charged jointly under Rule 8(b) or have been joined for trial under Rule 13; and

(B) the defendants are represented by the same counsel or counsel who are associated in law practice.

(2) Court's Responsibilities in Cases of Joint Representation. The court must promptly inquire about the propriety of joint representation and must personally advise each defendant of the right to the effective assistance of counsel, including separate representation. Unless there is good cause to believe that no conflict of interest is likely to arise, the court must take appropriate measures to protect each defendant's right to counsel.

Rule 45.   Computing and Extending Time

(a) **Computing Time.** The following rules apply in computing any time period specified in these rules, in any local rule or court order, or in any statute that does not specify a method of computing time.

(1) Period Stated in Days or a Longer Unit. When the period is stated in days or a longer unit of time:

(A) exclude the day of the event that triggers the period;

(B) count every day, including intermediate Saturdays, Sundays, and legal holidays; and

(C) include the last day of the period, but if the last day is a Saturday, Sunday, or legal holiday, the period continues to run until the end of the next day that is not a Saturday, Sunday, or legal holiday.

(2) Period Stated in Hours. When the period is stated in hours:

(A) begin counting immediately on the occurrence of the event that triggers the period;

(B) count every hour, including hours during intermediate Saturdays, Sundays, and legal holidays; and

(C) if the period would end on a Saturday, Sunday, or legal holiday, the period continues to run until the same time on the next day that is not a Saturday, Sunday, or legal holiday.

(3) Inaccessibility of the Clerk's Office. Unless the court orders otherwise, if the clerk's office is inaccessible:

(A) on the last day for filing under Rule 45(a)(1), then the time for filing is extended to the first accessible day that is not a Saturday, Sunday, or legal holiday; or

(B) during the last hour for filing under Rule 45(a)(2), then the time for filing is extended to the same time on the first accessible day that is not a Saturday, Sunday, or legal holiday.

(4) "Last Day" Defined. Unless a different time is set by a statute, local rule, or court order, the last day ends:

(A) for electronic filing, at midnight in the court's time zone; and

(B) for filing by other means, when the clerk's office is scheduled to close.

(5) "Next Day" Defined. The "next day" is determined by continuing to count forward when the period is measured after an event and backward when measured before an event.

(6) "Legal Holiday" Defined. "Legal holiday" means:

(A) the day set aside by statute for observing New Year's Day, Martin Luther King Jr.'s Birthday, Washington's Birthday, Memorial Day, Independence Day, Labor Day, Columbus Day, Veterans' Day, Thanksgiving Day, or Christmas Day;

(B) any day declared a holiday by the President or Congress; and

(C) for periods that are measured after an event, any other day declared a holiday by the state where the district court is located.

(b) Extending Time.

(1) In General. When an act must or may be done within a specified period, the court on its own may extend the time, or for good cause may do so on a party's motion made:

(A) before the originally prescribed or previously extended time expires; or

(B) after the time expires if the party failed to act because of excusable neglect.

(2) Exception. The court may not extend the time to take any action under Rule 35, except as stated in that rule.

(c) Additional Time After Certain Kinds of Service. Whenever a party must or may act within a specified time after being served and service is made under Rule 49(a)(4)(C), (D), and (E), 3 days are added after the period would otherwise expire under subdivision (a).

Rule 46.   Release from Custody; Supervising Detention

(a) Before Trial. The provisions of 18 U.S.C. §§3142 and 3144 govern pretrial release.

(b) During Trial. A person released before trial continues on release during trial under the same terms and conditions. But the court may order different terms and conditions or terminate the release if necessary to ensure that the person will be present during trial or that the person's conduct will not obstruct the orderly and expeditious progress of the trial.

(c) Pending Sentencing or Appeal. The provisions of 18 U.S.C. §3143 govern release pending sentencing or appeal. The burden of establishing that the defendant will not flee or pose a danger to any other person or to the community rests with the defendant.

(d) Pending Hearing on a Violation of Probation or Supervised Release. Rule 32.1(a)(6) governs release pending a hearing on a violation of probation or supervised release.

(e) Surety. The court must not approve a bond unless any surety appears to be qualified. Every surety, except a legally approved corporate surety, must demonstrate by affidavit that its assets are adequate. The court may require the affidavit to describe the following:

(1) the property that the surety proposes to use as security;

(2) any encumbrance on that property;

(3) the number and amount of any other undischarged bonds and bail undertakings the surety has issued; and

(4) any other liability of the surety.

(f) Bail Forfeiture.

(1) Declaration. The court must declare the bail forfeited if a condition of the bond is breached.

(2) Setting Aside. The court may set aside in whole or in part a bail forfeiture upon any condition the court may impose if:

(A) the surety later surrenders into custody the person released on the surety's appearance bond; or

(B) it appears that justice does not require bail forfeiture.

(3) Enforcement.

(A) Default Judgment and Execution. If it does not set aside a bail forfeiture, the court must, upon the government's motion, enter a default judgment.

(B) Jurisdiction and Service. By entering into a bond, each surety submits to the district court's jurisdiction and irrevocably appoints the district clerk as its agent to receive service of any filings affecting its liability.

(C) Motion to Enforce. The court may, upon the government's motion, enforce the surety's liability without an independent action. The government must serve any motion, and notice as the court prescribes, on the district clerk. If so served, the clerk must promptly mail a copy to the surety at its last known address.

(4) Remission. After entering a judgment under Rule 46(f)(3), the court may remit in whole or in part the judgment under the same conditions specified in Rule 46(f)(2).

(g) Exoneration. The court must exonerate the surety and release any bail when a bond condition has been satisfied or when the court has set aside or remitted the forfeiture. The court must exonerate a surety who deposits cash in the amount of the bond or timely surrenders the defendant into custody.

(h) Supervising Detention Pending Trial.

(1) In General. To eliminate unnecessary detention, the court must supervise the detention within the district of any defendants awaiting trial and of any persons held as material witnesses.

(2) Reports. An attorney for the government must report biweekly to the court, listing each material witness held in custody for more than 10 days pending indictment, arraignment, or trial. For each material witness listed in the report, an attorney for the government must state why the witness should not be released with or without a deposition being taken under Rule 15(a).

(i) Forfeiture of Property. The court may dispose of a charged offense by ordering the forfeiture of 18 U.S.C. §3142(c)(1)(B)(xi) property under 18 U.S.C. §3146(d), if a fine in the amount of the property's value would be an appropriate sentence for the charged offense.

(j) Producing a Statement.

(1) In General. Rule 26.2(a)-(d) and (f) applies at a detention hearing under 18 U.S.C. §3142, unless the court for good cause rules otherwise.

(2) Sanctions for Not Producing a Statement. If a party disobeys a Rule 26.2 order to produce a witness's statement, the court must not consider that witness's testimony at the detention hearing.

Rule 48.   Dismissal

(a) By the Government. The government may, with leave of court, dismiss an indictment, information, or complaint. The government may not dismiss the prosecution during trial without the defendant's consent.

(b) By the Court. The court may dismiss an indictment, information, or complaint if unnecessary delay occurs in:

(1) presenting a charge to a grand jury;

(2) filing an information against a defendant; or

(3) bringing a defendant to trial.

Rule 51. Preserving Claimed Error

(a) Exceptions Unnecessary. Exceptions to rulings or orders of the court are unnecessary.

(b) Preserving a Claim of Error. A party may preserve a claim of error by informing the court—when the court ruling or order is made or sought—of the action the party wishes the court to take, or the party's objection to the court's action and the grounds for that objection. If a party does not have an opportunity to object to a ruling or order, the absence of an objection does not later prejudice that party. A ruling or order that admits or excludes evidence is governed by Federal Rule of Evidence 103.

Rule 52. Harmless and Plain Error

(a) Harmless Error. Any error, defect, irregularity, or variance that does not affect substantial rights must be disregarded.

(b) Plain Error. A plain error that affects substantial rights may be considered even though it was not brought to the court's attention.

Wire and Electronic Communications Interception and Interception of Oral Communications Act

18 U.S.C. §2510. Definitions

As used in this chapter—

(1) "wire communication" means any aural transfer made in whole or in part through the use of facilities for the transmission of communications by the aid of wire, cable, or other like connection between the

point of origin and the point of reception (including the use of such connection in a switching station) furnished or operated by any person engaged in providing or operating such facilities for the transmission of interstate or foreign communications or communications affecting interstate or foreign commerce;

(2) "oral communication" means any oral communication uttered by a person exhibiting an expectation that such communication is not subject to interception under circumstances justifying such expectation, but such term does not include any electronic communication;

(3) "State" means any State of the United States, the District of Columbia, the Commonwealth of Puerto Rico, and any territory or possession of the United States;

(4) "intercept" means the aural or other acquisition of the contents of any wire, electronic, or oral communication through the use of any electronic, mechanical, or other device.

(5) "electronic, mechanical, or other device" means any device or apparatus which can be used to intercept a wire, oral, or electronic communication other than—

(a) any telephone or telegraph instrument, equipment or facility, or any component thereof,

(i) furnished to the subscriber or user by a provider of wire or electronic communication service in the ordinary course of its business and being used by the subscriber or user in the ordinary course of its business or furnished by such subscriber or user for connection to the facilities of such service and used in the ordinary course of its business; or

(ii) being used by a provider of wire or electronic communication service in the ordinary course of its business, or by an investigative or law enforcement officer in the ordinary course of his duties;

(b) a hearing aid or similar device being used to correct subnormal hearing to not better than normal;

(6) "person" means any employee, or agent of the United States or any State or political subdivision thereof, and any individual, partnership, association, joint stock company, trust, or corporation;

(7) "Investigative or law enforcement officer" means any officer of the United States or of a State or political subdivision thereof, who is empowered by law to conduct investigations of or to make arrests for offenses enumerated in this chapter, and any attorney authorized by law to prosecute or participate in the prosecution of such offenses;

(8) "contents," when used with respect to any wire, oral, or electronic communication, includes any information concerning the substance, purport, or meaning of that communication;

(9) "Judge of competent jurisdiction" means—

(a) a judge of a United States district court or a United States court of appeals; and

(b) a judge of any court of general criminal jurisdiction of a State who is authorized by a statute of that State to enter orders authorizing interceptions of wire, oral, or electronic communications;

(10) "communication common carrier" has the meaning given that term in section 3 of the Communications Act of 1934;

(11) "aggrieved person" means a person who was a party to any intercepted wire, oral, or electronic communication or a person against whom the interception was directed;

(12) "electronic communication" means any transfer of signs, signals, writing, images, sounds, data, or intelligence of any nature transmitted in whole or in part by a wire, radio, electromagnetic, photoelectronic or photooptical system that affects interstate or foreign commerce, but does not include—

(A) any wire or oral communication;

(B) any communication made through a tone-only paging device;

(C) any communication from a tracking device (as defined in section 3117 of this title); or

(D) electronic funds transfer information stored by a financial institution in a communications system used for the electronic storage and transfer of funds;

(13) "user" means any person or entity who—

(A) uses an electronic communication service; and

(B) is duly authorized by the provider of such service to engage in such use;

(14) "electronic communications system" means any wire, radio, electromagnetic, photooptical or photoelectronic facilities for the transmission of wire or electronic communications, and any computer facilities or related electronic equipment for the electronic storage of such communications;

(15) "electronic communication service" means any service which provides to users thereof the ability to send or receive wire or electronic communications;

(16) "readily accessible to the general public" means, with respect to a radio communication, that such communication is not—

(A) scrambled or encrypted;

(B) transmitted using modulation techniques whose essential parameters have been withheld from the public with the intention of preserving the privacy of such communication;

(C) carried on a subcarrier or other signal subsidiary to a radio transmission;

(D) transmitted over a communication system provided by a common carrier, unless the communication is a tone only paging system communication; or

(E) transmitted on frequencies allocated under part 25, subpart D, E, or F of part 74, or part 94 of the Rules of the Federal Communications Commission, unless, in the case of a communication transmitted on a frequency allocated under part 74 that is not exclusively allocated to broadcast auxiliary services, the communication is a two-way voice communication by radio;

(17) "electronic storage" means—

(A) any temporary, intermediate storage of a wire or electronic communication incidental to the electronic transmission thereof; and

(B) any storage of such communication by an electronic communication service for purposes of backup protection of such communication;

(18) "aural transfer" means a transfer containing the human voice at any point between and including the point of origin and the point of reception;

(19) "foreign intelligence information," for purposes of section 2517(6) of this title, means—

(A) information, whether or not concerning a United States person, that relates to the ability of the United States to protect against—

(i) actual or potential attack or other grave hostile acts of a foreign power or an agent of a foreign power;

(ii) sabotage or international terrorism by a foreign power or an agent of a foreign power; or

(iii) clandestine intelligence activities by an intelligence service or network of a foreign power or by an agent of a foreign power; or

(B) information, whether or not concerning a United States person, with respect to a foreign power or foreign territory that relates to—

(i) the national defense or the security of the United States; or

(ii) the conduct of the foreign affairs of the United States;

(20) "protected computer" has the meaning set forth in section 1030; and

(21) "computer trespasser" —

(A) means a person who accesses a protected computer without authorization and thus has no reasonable expectation of privacy in any communication transmitted to, through, or from the protected computer; and

(B) does not include a person known by the owner or operator of the protected computer to have an existing contractual relationship with the owner or operator of the protected computer for access to all or part of the protected computer.

18 U.S.C. §2511. Interception and Disclosure of Wire, Oral, or Electronic Communications Prohibited

(1) Except as otherwise specifically provided in this chapter any person who—

(a) intentionally intercepts, endeavors to intercept, or procures any other person to intercept or endeavor to intercept, any wire, oral, or electronic communication;

(b) intentionally uses, endeavors to use, or procures any other person to use or endeavor to use any electronic, mechanical, or other device to intercept any oral communication when—

(i) such device is affixed to, or otherwise transmits a signal through, a wire, cable, or other like connection used in wire communication; or

(ii) such device transmits communications by radio, or interferes with the transmission of such communication; or

(iii) such person knows, or has reason to know, that such device or any component thereof has been sent through the mail or transported in interstate or foreign commerce; or

(iv) such use or endeavor to use (A) takes place on the premises of any business or other commercial establishment the operations of which affect interstate or foreign commerce; or (B) obtains or is for the purpose of obtaining information relating to the operations of any business or other commercial establishment the operations of which affect interstate or foreign commerce; or

(v) such person acts in the District of Columbia, the Commonwealth of Puerto Rico, or any territory or possession of the United States;

(c) intentionally discloses, or endeavors to disclose, to any other person the contents of any wire, oral, or electronic communication, knowing or having reason to know that the information was obtained through the interception of a wire, oral, or electronic communication in violation of this subsection;

(d) intentionally uses, or endeavors to use, the contents of any wire, oral, or electronic communication, knowing or having reason to know that the information was obtained through the interception of a wire, oral, or electronic communication in violation of this subsection; or

(e)(i) intentionally discloses, or endeavors to disclose, to any other person the contents of any wire, oral, or electronic communication, intercepted by means authorized by sections 2511(2)(a)(ii), 2511(2)(b)-(c), 2511(2)(e), 2516, and 2518 of this chapter,

(ii) knowing or having reason to know that the information was obtained through the interception of such a communication in connection with a criminal investigation,

(iii) having obtained or received the information in connection with a criminal investigation, and

(iv) with intent to improperly obstruct, impede, or interfere with a duly authorized criminal investigation, shall be punished as provided in subsection (4) or shall be subject to suit as provided in subsection (5).

(2)(a)(i) It shall not be unlawful under this chapter for an operator of a switchboard, or an officer, employee, or agent of a provider of wire or electronic communication service, whose facilities are used in the transmission of a wire or electronic communication, to intercept, disclose, or use that communication in the normal course of his employment while engaged in any activity which is a necessary incident to the rendition of his service or to the protection of the rights or property of the provider of that service, except that a provider of wire communication service to the public shall not utilize service observing or random monitoring except for mechanical or service quality control checks.

(ii) Notwithstanding any other law, providers of wire or electronic communication service, their officers, employees, and agents, landlords, custodians, or other persons, are authorized to provide information, facilities, or technical assistance to persons authorized by law to intercept wire, oral, or electronic communications or to conduct electronic surveillance, as defined in section 101 of the Foreign Intelligence Surveillance Act of 1978, if such provider, its officers, employees, or agents, landlord, custodian, or other specified person, has been provided with —

(A) a court order directing such assistance or a court order pursuant to section 704 of the Foreign Intelligence Surveillance Act of 1978 signed by the authorizing judge, or

(B) a certification in writing by a person specified in section 2518(7) of this title or the Attorney General of the United States that no warrant or court order is required by law, that all statutory requirements have been met, and that the specified assistance is required, setting forth the period of time during which the provision of the information, facilities, or technical assistance is authorized and specifying the information, facilities, or technical assistance required. No provider of wire or electronic communication service, officer, employee, or agent thereof, or landlord, custodian, or other specified person shall disclose the existence of any interception or surveillance or the device used to accomplish the interception or surveillance with respect to which the person has been furnished a court order or certification under this chapter, except as may otherwise be required by legal process and then only after prior notification to the Attorney General or to the principal prosecuting attorney of a State or any political subdivision of a State, as may be appropriate. Any such disclosure, shall render such person liable for the civil damages provided for in section 2520. No cause of action shall lie in any court against any provider of wire or electronic communication service, its officers, employees, or agents, landlord, custodian, or other specified person for providing information, facilities, or assistance in accordance with the terms of a court order, statutory authorization, or certification under this chapter.

(iii) If a certification under subparagraph (ii)(B) for assistance to obtain foreign intelligence information is based on statutory authority, the certification shall identify the specific statutory provision and shall certify that the statutory requirements have been met.

(b) It shall not be unlawful under this chapter for an officer, employee, or agent of the Federal Communications Commission, in the normal course of his employment and in discharge of the monitoring responsibilities exercised by the Commission in the enforcement of chapter 5 of title 47 of the United States Code, to intercept a wire or electronic communication, or oral communication transmitted by radio, or to disclose or use the information thereby obtained.

(c) It shall not be unlawful under this chapter for a person acting under color of law to intercept a wire, oral, or electronic communication, where such person is a party to the communication or one of the parties to the communication has given prior consent to such interception.

(d) It shall not be unlawful under this chapter for a person not acting under color of law to intercept a wire, oral, or electronic communication where such person is a party to the communication or where one of the parties to the communication has given prior consent to such interception unless such communication is intercepted for the purpose of committing any criminal or tortious act in violation of the Constitution or laws of the United States or of any State.

(e) Notwithstanding any other provision of this title or section 705 or 706 of the Communications Act of 1934, it shall not be unlawful for an officer, employee, or agent of the United States in the normal course of his official duty to conduct electronic surveillance, as defined in section 101 of the Foreign Intelligence Surveillance Act of 1978, as authorized by that Act.

(f) Nothing contained in this chapter or chapter 121 or 206 of this title, or section 705 of the Communications Act of 1934, shall be deemed to affect the acquisition by the United States Government of foreign intelligence information from international or foreign communications, or foreign intelligence activities conducted in accordance with otherwise applicable Federal law involving a foreign electronic communications system, utilizing a means other than electronic surveillance as defined in section 101 of the Foreign Intelligence Surveillance Act of 1978, and procedures in this chapter or chapter 121 and the Foreign Intelligence Surveillance Act of 1978 shall be the exclusive means by which electronic surveillance, as defined in section 101 of such Act, and the interception of domestic wire, oral, and electronic communications may be conducted.

(g) It shall not be unlawful under this chapter or chapter 121 of this title for any person—

(i) to intercept or access an electronic communication made through an electronic communication system that is configured so that such electronic communication is readily accessible to the general public;

(ii) to intercept any radio communication which is transmitted—

(I) by any station for the use of the general public, or that relates to ships, aircraft, vehicles, or persons in distress;

(II) by any governmental, law enforcement, civil defense, private land mobile, or public safety communications system, including police and fire, readily accessible to the general public;

(III) by a station operating on an authorized frequency within the bands allocated to the amateur, citizens band, or general mobile radio services; or

(IV) by any marine or aeronautical communications system;

(iii) to engage in any conduct which—

(I) is prohibited by section 633 of the Communications Act of 1934; or

(II) is excepted from the application of section 705(a) of the Communications Act of 1934 by section 705(b) of that Act;

(iv) to intercept any wire or electronic communication the transmission of which is causing harmful interference to any lawfully operating station or consumer electronic equipment, to the extent necessary to identify the source of such interference; or

(v) for other users of the same frequency to intercept any radio communication made through a system that utilizes frequencies monitored by individuals engaged in the provision or the use of such system, if such communication is not scrambled or encrypted.

(h) It shall not be unlawful under this chapter—

(i) to use a pen register or a trap and trace device (as those terms are defined for the purposes of chapter 206 (relating to pen registers and trap and trace devices) of this title); or

(ii) for a provider of electronic communication service to record the fact that a wire or electronic communication was initiated or completed in order to protect such provider, another provider furnishing service toward the completion of the wire or electronic communication, or a user of that service, from fraudulent, unlawful or abusive use of such service.

(i) It shall not be unlawful under this chapter for a person acting under color of law to intercept the wire or electronic communications of a computer trespasser transmitted to, through, or from the protected computer, if—

      (I) the owner or operator of the protected computer authorizes the interception of the computer trespasser's communications on the protected computer;

      (II) the person acting under color of law is lawfully engaged in an investigation;

      (III) the person acting under color of law has reasonable grounds to believe that the contents of the computer trespasser's communications will be relevant to the investigation; and

      (IV) such interception does not acquire communications other than those transmitted to or from the computer trespasser.

(j) It shall not be unlawful under this chapter for a provider of electronic communication service to the public or remote computing service to intercept or disclose the contents of a wire or electronic communication in response to an order from a foreign government that is subject to an executive agreement that the Attorney General has determined and certified to Congress satisfies section 2523.

(3)(a) Except as provided in paragraph (b) of this subsection, a person or entity providing an electronic communication service to the public shall not intentionally divulge the contents of any communication (other than one to such person or entity, or an agent thereof) while in transmission on that service to any person or entity other than an addressee or intended recipient of such communication or an agent of such addressee or intended recipient.

    (b) A person or entity providing electronic communication service to the public may divulge the contents of any such communication—

      (i) as otherwise authorized in section 2511(2)(a) or 2517 of this title;

      (ii) with the lawful consent of the originator or any addressee or intended recipient of such communication;

      (iii) to a person employed or authorized, or whose facilities are used, to forward such communication to its destination; or

      (iv) which were inadvertently obtained by the service provider and which appear to pertain to the commission of a crime, if such divulgence is made to a law enforcement agency.

(4)(a) Except as provided in paragraph (b) of this subsection or in subsection (5), whoever violates subsection (1) of this section shall be fined under this title or imprisoned not more than five years, or both.

(b) Conduct otherwise an offense under this subsection that consists of or relates to the interception of a satellite transmission that is not encrypted or scrambled and that is transmitted—

(i) to a broadcasting station for purposes of retransmission to the general public; or

(ii) as an audio subcarrier intended for redistribution to facilities open to the public, but not including data transmissions or telephone calls, is not an offense under this subsection unless the conduct is for the purposes of direct or indirect commercial advantage or private financial gain.

(5)(a)(i) If the communication is—

(A) a private satellite video communication that is not scrambled or encrypted and the conduct in violation of this chapter is the private viewing of that communication and is not for a tortious or illegal purpose or for purposes of direct or indirect commercial advantage or private commercial gain; or

(B) a radio communication that is transmitted on frequencies allocated under subpart D of part 74 of the rules of the Federal Communications Commission that is not scrambled or encrypted and the conduct in violation of this chapter is not for a tortious or illegal purpose or for purposes of direct or indirect commercial advantage or private commercial gain, then the person who engages in such conduct shall be subject to suit by the Federal Government in a court of competent jurisdiction.

(ii) In an action under this subsection—

(A) if the violation of this chapter is a first offense for the person under paragraph (a) of subsection (4) and such person has not been found liable in a civil action under section 2520 of this title, the Federal Government shall be entitled to appropriate injunctive relief; and

(B) if the violation of this chapter is a second or subsequent offense under paragraph (a) of subsection (4) or such person has been found liable in any prior civil action under section 2520, the person shall be subject to a mandatory $500 civil fine.

(b) The court may use any means within its authority to enforce an injunction issued under paragraph (ii)(A), and shall impose a civil fine of not less than $500 for each violation of such an injunction.

18 U.S.C. §2515.   Prohibition of Use as Evidence of Intercepted Wire or Oral Communications

Whenever any wire or oral communication has been intercepted, no part of the contents of such communication and no evidence derived therefrom may be received in evidence in any trial, hearing, or other proceeding in or before any court, grand jury, department, officer, agency, regulatory body, legislative committee, or other authority of the United States, a State, or a political subdivision thereof if the disclosure of that information would be in violation of this chapter.

Bail Reform Act of 1984 (as amended)

18 U.S.C. §3141.   Release and Detention Authority Generally

(a) Pending trial. A judicial officer authorized to order the arrest of a person under section 3041 of this title before whom an arrested person is brought shall order that such person be released or detained, pending judicial proceedings, under this chapter [18 U.S.C. §§ 3141 et seq.].

(b) Pending sentence or appeal. A judicial officer of a court of original jurisdiction over an offense, or a judicial officer of a Federal appellate court, shall order that, pending imposition or execution of sentence, or pending appeal of conviction or sentence, a person be released or detained under this chapter [18 U.S.C. §§ 3141 et seq.].

18 U.S.C. §3142.   Release or Detention of a Defendant Pending Trial

(a) In general. Upon the appearance before a judicial officer of a person charged with an offense, the judicial officer shall issue an order that, pending trial, the person be—

(1) Released on personal recognizance or upon execution of an unsecured appearance bond, under subsection (b) of this section;

(2) released on a condition or combination of conditions under subsection (c) of this section;

(3) temporarily detained to permit revocation of conditional release, deportation, or exclusion under subsection (d) of this section; or

(4) detained under subsection (e) of this section.

(b) Release on personal recognizance or unsecured appearance bond. The judicial officer shall order the pretrial release of the person on personal recognizance, or upon execution of an unsecured appearance bond in an amount specified by the court, subject to the condition that the person not commit a Federal, State, or local crime during the period of release, unless the judicial officer determines that such release will not reasonably assure the appearance of the person as required or will endanger the safety of any other person or the community.

(c) Release on conditions.

(1) If the judicial officer determines that the release described in subsection (b) of this section will not reasonably assure the appearance of the person as required or will endanger the safety of any other person or the community, such judicial officer shall order the pretrial release of the person—

(A) subject to the condition that the person not commit a Federal, State, or local crime during the period of release; and

(B) subject to the least restrictive further condition, or combination of conditions, that such judicial officer determines will reasonably assure the appearance of the person as required and the safety of any other person and the community, which may include the condition that the person—

(i) remain in the custody of a designated person, who agrees to assume supervision and to report any violation of a release condition to the court, if the designated person is able reasonably to assure the judicial officer that the person will appear as required and will not pose a danger to the safety of any other person or the community;

(ii) maintain employment, or, if unemployed, actively seek employment;

(iii) maintain or commence an educational program;

(iv) abide by specified restrictions on personal associations, place of abode, or travel;

(v) avoid all contact with an alleged victim of the crime and with a potential witness who may testify concerning the offense;

(vi) report on a regular basis to a designated law enforcement agency, pretrial services agency, or other agency;

(vii) comply with a specified curfew;

(viii) refrain from possessing a firearm, destructive device, or other dangerous weapon;

(ix) refrain from excessive use of alcohol, or any use of a narcotic drug or other controlled substance, as defined in section 102 of the Controlled Substances Act (21 U.S.C. § 802), without a prescription by a licensed medical practitioner;

(x) undergo available medical, psychological, or psychiatric treatment, including treatment for drug or alcohol dependency, and remain in a specified institution if required for that purpose;

(xi) execute an agreement to forfeit, upon failing to appear as required, property of a sufficient unencumbered value, including money, as is reasonably necessary to assure the appearance of the person as required, and shall provide the court with proof of ownership and the value of the property along with information regarding existing encumbrances as the judicial office may require;

(xii) execute a bail bond with solvent sureties; who will execute an agreement to forfeit in such amount as is reasonably necessary to assure appearance of the person as required and shall provide the court with information regarding the value of the assets and liabilities of the surety if other than an approved surety and the nature and extent of encumbrances against the surety's property; such surety shall have a net worth which shall have sufficient unencumbered value to pay the amount of the bail bond;

(xiii) return to custody for specified hours following release for employment, schooling, or other limited purposes; and

(xiv) satisfy any other condition that is reasonably necessary to assure the appearance of the person as required and to assure the safety of any other person and the community.

In any case that involves a minor victim under section 1201, 1591, 2241, 2242, 2244(a)(1), 2245, 2251, 2251A, 2252(a)(1), 2252(a)(2), 2252(a)(3), 2252A(a)(1), 2252A(a)(2), 2252A(a)(3), 2252A(a)(4), 2260, 2421, 2422, 2423, or 2425 of this title, or a failure to register offense under section 2250 of this title, any release order shall contain, at a minimum, a condition of electronic monitoring and each of the conditions specified at subparagraphs (iv), (v), (vi), (vii), and (viii).

(2) The judicial officer may not impose a financial condition that results in the pretrial detention of the person.

(3) The judicial officer may at any time amend the order to impose additional or different conditions of release.

(d) Temporary detention to permit revocation of conditional release, deportation, or exclusion. If the judicial officer determines that—

(1) such person—

(A) is, and was at the time the offense was committed, on—

(i) release pending trial for a felony under Federal, State, or local law;

(ii) release pending imposition or execution of sentence, appeal of sentence or conviction, or completion of sentence, for any offense under Federal, State, or local law; or

(iii) probation or parole for any offense under Federal, State, or local law; or

(B) is not a citizen of the United States or lawfully admitted for permanent residence, as defined in section 101(a)(20) of the Immigration and Nationality Act (8 U.S.C. § 1101(a)(20)); and

(2) the person may flee or pose a danger to any other person or the community; such judicial officer shall order the detention of the person, for a period of not more than ten days, excluding Saturdays, Sundays, and holidays, and direct the attorney for the Government to notify the appropriate court, probation or parole official, or State or local law enforcement official, or the appropriate official of the Immigration and Naturalization Service. If the official fails or declines to take the person into custody during that period, the person shall be treated in accordance with the other provisions of this section, notwithstanding the applicability of other provisions of law governing release pending trial or deportation or exclusion proceedings. If temporary detention is sought under paragraph (1)(B) of this subsection, the person has the burden of proving to the court such person's United States citizenship or lawful admission for permanent residence.

(e) Detention.

(1) If, after a hearing pursuant to the provisions of subsection (f) of this section, the judicial officer finds that no condition or combination of conditions will reasonably assure the appearance of the person as required and the safety of any other person and the community, such judicial officer shall order the detention of the person before trial.

(2) In a case described in subsection (f)(l) of this section, a rebuttable presumption arises that no condition or combination of conditions will reasonably assure the safety of any other person and the community if such judicial officer finds that—

(A) the person has been convicted of a Federal offense that is described in subsection (f)(l) of this section, or of a State or local offense that would have been an offense described in subsection (f)(l) of this section if a circumstance giving rise to Federal jurisdiction had existed;

(B) the offense described in subparagraph (A) was committed while the person was on release pending trial for a Federal, State, or local offense; and

(C) a period of not more than five years has elapsed since the date of conviction, or the release of the person from imprisonment, for the offense described in subparagraph (A), whichever is later.

(3) Subject to rebuttal by the person, it shall be presumed that no condition or combination of conditions will reasonably assure the appearance of the person as required and the safety of the community if the judicial officer finds that there is probable cause to believe that the person committed—

(A) an offense for which a maximum term of imprisonment of ten years or more is prescribed in the Controlled Substances Act (21 U.S.C. §§ 801 et seq.), the Controlled Substances Import and Export Act (21 U.S.C. §§ 951 et seq.), or chapter 705 of title 46;

(B) an offense under section 924(c), 956(a), or 2332b of this title;

(C) an offense listed in section 2332b(g)(5)(B) of title 18, United States Code, for which a maximum term of imprisonment of 10 years or more is prescribed;

(D) an offense under chapter 77 of this title for which a maximum term of imprisonment of 20 years or more is prescribed; or

(E) an offense involving a minor victim under section 1201, 1591, 2241, 2242, 2244(a)(1), 2245, 2251, 2251A, 2252(a)(1), 2252(a)(2), 2252(a)(3), 2252A(a)(1), 2252A(a)(2), 2252A(a)(3), 2252A(a)(4), 2260, 2421, 2422, 2423, or 2425 of this title.

(f) Detention hearing. The judicial officer shall hold a hearing to determine whether any condition or combination of conditions set forth in subsection (c) of this section will reasonably assure the appearance of the person as required and the safety of any other person and the community—

(1) upon motion of the attorney for the Government, in a case that involves—

(A) a crime of violence;

(B) an offense for which the maximum sentence is life imprisonment or death;

(C) an offense for which a maximum term of imprisonment of ten years or more is prescribed in the Controlled Substances Act (21 U.S.C. §§ 801 et seq.), the Controlled Substances Import and Export Act (21 U.S.C. §§ 951 et seq.), or the Maritime Drug Law Enforcement Act (46 U.S.C. App. §§ 1901 et seq.); or

(D) any felony if the person has been convicted of two or more offenses described in subparagraphs (A) through (C) of this paragraph, or two or more State or local offenses that would have been offenses described in subparagraphs (A) through (C) of this paragraph if a circumstance giving rise to Federal jurisdiction had existed, or a combination of such offenses; or

(2) upon motion of the attorney for the Government or upon the judicial officer's own motion, in a case that involves—

(A) a serious risk that such person will flee; or

(B) a serious risk that the person will obstruct or attempt to obstruct justice, or threaten, injure, or intimidate, or attempt to threaten, injure, or intimidate, a prospective witness or juror.

The hearing shall be held immediately upon the person's first appearance before the judicial officer unless that person, or the attorney for the Government, seeks a continuance. Except for good cause, a continuance on motion of the person may not exceed five days (not including any intermediate Saturday, Sunday, or legal holiday), and a continuance on motion of the attorney for the Government may not exceed three days (not including any intermediate Saturday, Sunday, or legal holiday). During a continuance, the person shall be detained and the judicial officer, on motion of the attorney for the Government or sua sponte, may order that, while in custody, a person who appears to be a narcotics addict receive a medical examination to determine whether such person is an addict. At the hearing, the person has the right to be represented by counsel and, if financially unable to obtain adequate representation, to have counsel appointed. The person shall be afforded an opportunity to testify, to present witnesses, to cross-examine witnesses who appear at the hearing, and to present information by proffer or otherwise. The rules concerning admissibility of evidence in criminal trials do not apply to the presentation and consideration of information at the hearing. The facts the judicial officer uses to support a finding pursuant to subsection (e) that no condition or combination of conditions will reasonably assure the safety of any other person and the community shall be supported by clear and convincing evidence. The person may be detained pending completion of the hearing. The hearing may be reopened, before or after a determination by the judicial officer, at any time before trial if the judicial officer finds that information exists that was not known to the movant at the time of the hearing and that has a material bearing on the issue whether there are conditions of release that will reasonably assure the appearance of the person as required and the safety of any other person and the community.

(g) Factors to be considered. The judicial officer shall, in determining whether there are conditions of release that will reasonably assure the appearance of the person as required and the safety of any other person and the community, take into account the available information concerning—

(1) the nature and circumstances of the offense charged, including whether the offense is a crime of violence or involves a narcotic drug;

(2) the weight of the evidence against the person;

(3) the history and characteristics of the person, including—

(A) the person's character, physical and mental condition, family ties, employment, financial resources, length of residence in the community, community ties, past conduct, history relating to drug or alcohol abuse, criminal history, and record concerning appearance at court proceedings; and

(B) whether, at the time of the current offense or arrest, the person was on probation, on parole, or on other release pending trial, sentencing, appeal, or completion of sentence for an offense under Federal, State, or local law; and

(4) the nature and seriousness of the danger to any person or the community that would be posed by the person's release. In considering the conditions of release described in subsection (c)(1)(B)(xi) or (c)(1)(B)(xii) of this section, the judicial officer may, upon his own motion, or shall, upon the motion of the Government, conduct an inquiry into the source of the property to be designated for potential forfeiture or offered as collateral to secure a bond, and shall decline to accept the designation, or the use as collateral, of property that, because of its source, will not reasonably assure the appearance of the person as required.

(h) Contents of release order. In a release order issued under subsection (b) or (c) of this section, the judicial officer shall—

(1) include a written statement that sets forth all the conditions to which the release is subject, in a manner sufficiently clear and specific to serve as a guide for the person's conduct; and

(2) advise the person of—

(A) the penalties for violating a condition of release, including the penalties for committing an offense while on pretrial release;

(B) the consequences of violating a condition of release, including the immediate issuance of a warrant for the person's arrest; and

(C) sections 1503 of this title (relating to intimidation of witnesses, jurors, and officers of the court), 1510 (relating to obstruction of criminal investigations), 1512 (tampering with a witness, victim, or an informant), and 1513 (retaliating against a witness, victim, or an informant).

(i) Contents of detention order. In a detention order issued under subsection (e) of this section, the judicial officer shall—

(1) include written findings of fact and a written statement of the reasons for the detention;

(2) direct that the person be committed to the custody of the Attorney General for confinement in a corrections facility separate, to the extent practicable, from persons awaiting or serving sentences or being held in custody pending appeal;

(3) direct that the person be afforded reasonable opportunity for private consultation with counsel; and

(4) direct that, on order of a court of the United States or on request of an attorney for the Government, the person in charge of the corrections facility in which the person is confined deliver the person to a United States marshal for the purpose of an appearance in connection with a court proceeding.

The judicial officer may, by subsequent order, permit the temporary release of the person, in the custody of a United States marshal or another appropriate person, to the extent that the judicial officer determines such release to be necessary for preparation of the person's defense or for another compelling reason.

(j) Presumption of innocence. Nothing in this section shall be construed as modifying or limiting the presumption of innocence.

18 U.S.C. §3143. Release or Detention of a Defendant Pending Sentence or Appeal

(a) Release or detention pending sentence.

(1) Except as provided in paragraph (2), the judicial officer shall order that a person who has been found guilty of an offense and who is awaiting imposition or execution of sentence, other than a person for whom the applicable guideline promulgated pursuant to 28 U.S.C. § 994 does not recommend a term of imprisonment, be detained, unless the judicial officer finds by clear and convincing evidence that the person is not likely to flee or pose a danger to the safety of any other person or the community if released under section 3142(b) or (c). If the judicial officer makes such a finding, such judicial officer shall order the release of the person in accordance with section 3142(b) or (c).

(2) The judicial officer shall order that a person who has been found guilty of an offense in a case described in subparagraph (A), (B), or (C) of subsection (f)(1) of section 3142 and is awaiting imposition or execution of sentence be detained unless—

(A) (i) the judicial officer finds there is a substantial likelihood that a motion for acquittal or new trial will be granted; or

(ii) an attorney for the Government has recommended that no sentence of imprisonment be imposed on the person; and

(B) the judicial officer finds by clear and convincing evidence that the person is not likely to flee or pose a danger to any other person or the community.

(b) Release or detention pending appeal by the defendant.

(1) Except as provided in paragraph (2), the judicial officer shall order that a person who has been found guilty of an offense and sentenced to a term of imprisonment, and who has filed an appeal or a petition for a writ of certiorari, be detained, unless the judicial officer finds—

(A) by clear and convincing evidence that the person is not likely to flee or pose a danger to the safety of any other person or the community if released under section 3142(b) or (c) of this title; and

(B) that the appeal is not for the purpose of delay and raises a substantial question of law or fact likely to result in—

(i) reversal

(ii) an order for a new trial,

(iii) a sentence that does not include a term of imprisonment, or

(iv) a reduced sentence to a term of imprisonment less than the total of the time already served plus the expected duration of the appeal process.

If the judicial officer makes such findings, such judicial officer shall order the release of the person in accordance with section 3142(b) or (c) of this title, except that in the circumstance described in subparagraph (B)(iv) of this paragraph, the judicial officer shall order the detention terminated at the expiration of the likely reduced sentence.

(2) The judicial officer shall order that a person who has been found guilty of an offense in a case described in subparagraph (A), (B), or (C) of subsection (f)(1) of section 3142 and sentenced to a term of imprisonment, and who has filed an appeal or a petition for a writ of certiorari, be detained.

(c) Release or detention pending appeal by the government. The judicial officer shall treat a defendant in a case in which an appeal has been taken by the United States under section 3731 of this title, in accordance with section 3142 of this title, unless the defendant is otherwise subject to a release or detention order. Except as provided in subsection (b) of this section, the judicial officer, in a case in which an appeal has been taken by the United States under section 3742, shall—

(1) if the person has been sentenced to a term of imprisonment, order that person detained; and

(2) in any other circumstance, release or detain the person under section 3142.

18 U.S.C. §3144. Release or Detention of a Material Witness

If it appears from an affidavit filed by a party that the testimony of a person is material in a criminal proceeding, and if it is shown that it may become impracticable to secure the presence of the person by subpoena, a judicial officer may order the arrest of the person and treat the person in accordance with the provisions of section 3142 of this title. No material witness may be detained because of inability to comply with any condition of release if the testimony of such witness can adequately be secured by deposition, and if further detention is not necessary to prevent a failure of justice. Release of a material witness may be delayed for a reasonable period of time until the deposition of the witness can be taken pursuant to the Federal Rules of Criminal Procedure.

18 U.S.C. §3145. Review and Appeal of a Release or Detention Order

(a) Review of a release order. If a person is ordered released by a magistrate [United States magistrate judge], or by a person other than a judge of a court having original jurisdiction over the offense and other than a Federal appellate court—

(1) the attorney for the Government may file, with the court having original jurisdiction over the offense, a motion for revocation of the order or amendment of the conditions of release; and

(2) the person may file, with the court having original jurisdiction over the offense, a motion for amendment of the conditions of release. The motion shall be determined promptly.

(b) Review of a detention order. If a person is ordered detained by a magistrate [United States magistrate judge], or by a person other than a judge of a court having original jurisdiction over the offense and other than a Federal appellate court, the person may file, with the court having original jurisdiction over the offense, a motion for revocation or amendment of the order. The motion shall be determined promptly.

(c) Appeal from a release or detention order. An appeal from a release or detention order, or from a decision denying revocation or amendment of such an order, is governed by the provisions of section 1291 of title 28 and section 3731 of this title. The appeal shall be determined promptly. A person subject to detention pursuant to section 3143(a)(2) or (b)(2), and who meets the conditions of release set forth in section 3143(a)(1) or (b)(1), may be ordered released, under appropriate conditions, by the judicial officer if it is clearly shown that there are exceptional reasons why such person's detention would not be appropriate.

18 U.S.C. §3146. Penalty for Failure to Appear

(a) Offense. Whoever, having been released under this chapter [18 U.S.C. §§ 3141 et seq.] knowingly—

(1) fails to appear before a court as required by the conditions of release; or

(2) fails to surrender for service of sentence pursuant to a court order; shall be punished as provided in subsection (b) of this section.

(b) Punishment.

(1) The punishment for an offense under this section is—

(A) if the person was released in connection with a charge of, or while awaiting sentence, surrender for service of sentence, or appeal or certiorari after conviction for—

(i) an offense punishable by death, life imprisonment, or imprisonment for a term of 15 years or more, a fine under this title or imprisonment for not more than ten years, or both;

(ii) an offense punishable by imprisonment for a term of five years or more, a fine under this title or imprisonment for not more than five years, or both;

(iii) any other felony, a fine under this title or imprisonment for not more than two years, or both; or

(iv) a misdemeanor, a fine under this title or imprisonment for not more than one year, or both; and

(B) if the person was released for appearance as a material witness, a fine under this chapter [18 U.S.C. §§ 3141 et seq.] or imprisonment for not more than one year, or both.

(2) A term of imprisonment imposed under this section shall be consecutive to the sentence of imprisonment for any other offense.

(c) Affirmative defense. It is an affirmative defense to a prosecution under this section that uncontrollable circumstances prevented the person from appearing or surrendering, and that the person did not contribute to the creation of such circumstances in reckless disregard of the requirement to appear or surrender, and that the person appeared or surrendered as soon as such circumstances ceased to exist.

(d) Declaration of forfeiture. If a person fails to appear before a court as required, and the person executed an appearance bond pursuant to section 3142(b) of this title or is subject to the release condition set forth in clause (xi) or (xii) of section 3142(c)(1)(B) of this title, the judicial officer may, regardless of whether the person has been charged with an offense under this section, declare any property designated pursuant to that section to be forfeited to the United States.

18 U.S.C. §3147. Penalty for an Offense Committed While on Release

A person convicted of an offense committed while released under this chapter [18 U.S.C. §§ 3141 et seq.] shall be sentenced, in addition to the sentence prescribed for the offense, to—

(1) a term of imprisonment of not more than ten years if the offense is a felony; or

(2) a term of imprisonment of not more than one year if the offense is a misdemeanor.

A term of imprisonment imposed under this section shall be consecutive to any other sentence of imprisonment.

18 U.S.C. §3148.   Sanctions for Violation of a Release Condition

(a) Available sanctions. A person who has been released pursuant to the provisions of section 3142 of this title, and who has violated a condition of his release, is subject to a revocation of release, an order of detention, and a prosecution for contempt of court.

(b) Revocation of release. The attorney for the Government may initiate a proceeding for revocation of an order of release by filing a motion with the district court. A judicial officer may issue a warrant for the arrest of a person charged with violating a condition of release, and the person shall be brought before a judicial officer in the district in which such person's arrest was ordered for a proceeding in accordance with this section. To the extent practicable, a person charged with violating the condition of release that such person not commit a Federal, State, or local crime during the period of release, shall be brought before the judicial officer who ordered the release and whose order is alleged to have been violated. The judicial officer shall enter an order of revocation and detention if, after a hearing, the judicial officer—

(1) finds that there is—

(A) probable cause to believe that the person has committed a Federal, State, or local crime while on release; or

(B) clear and convincing evidence that the person has violated any other condition of release; and

(2) finds that—

(A) based on the factors set forth in section 3142(g) of this title, there is no condition or combination of conditions of release that will assure that the person will not flee or pose a danger to the safety of any other person or the community; or

(B) the person is unlikely to abide by any condition or combination of conditions of release.

If there is probable cause to believe that, while on release, the person committed a Federal, State, or local felony, a rebuttable presumption arises that no condition or combination of conditions will assure that the person will not pose a danger to the safety of any other person or the community. If the judicial officer finds that there are conditions of release that will assure that the person will not flee or pose a danger to the safety of any other person or the community, and that the person will abide by such conditions, the judicial officer shall treat the person in accordance with the provisions of section 3142 of this title and may amend the conditions of release accordingly.

(c) Prosecution for contempt. The judicial officer may commence a prosecution for contempt, under section 401 of this title, if the person has violated a condition of release.

18 U.S.C. §3149. Surrender of an Offender by a Surety

A person charged with an offense, who is released upon the execution of an appearance bond with a surety, may be arrested by the surety, and if so arrested, shall be delivered promptly to a United States marshal and brought before a judicial officer. The judicial officer shall determine in accordance with the provisions of section 3148(b) whether to revoke the release of the person, and may absolve the surety of responsibility to pay all or part of the bond in accordance with the provisions of Rule 46 of the Federal Rules of Criminal Procedure. The person so committed shall be held in official detention until released pursuant to this chapter [18 U.S.C. §§ 3141 et seq.] or another provision of law.

18 U.S.C. §3150. Applicability to a Case Removed from a State Court

The provisions of this chapter [18 U.S.C. §§ 3141 et seq.] apply to a criminal case removed to a Federal court from a State court.

Speedy Trial Act of 1974 (as amended)

18 U.S.C. §3161.   Time Limits and Exclusions

(a) In any case involving a defendant charged with an offense, the appropriate judicial officer, at the earliest practicable time, shall, after consultation with the counsel for the defendant and the attorney for the Government, set the case for trial on a day certain, or list it for trial on a weekly or other short-term trial calendar at a place within the judicial district, so as to assure a speedy trial.

(b) Any information or indictment charging an individual with the commission of an offense shall be filed within thirty days from the date on which such individual was arrested or served with a summons in connection with such charges. If an individual has been charged with a felony in a district in which no grand jury has been in session during such thirty-day period, the period of time for filing of the indictment shall be extended an additional thirty days.

(c)(1) In any case in which a plea of not guilty is entered, the trial of a defendant charged in an information or indictment with the commission of an offense shall commence within seventy days from the filing date (and making public) of the information or indictment, or from the date the defendant has appeared before a judicial officer of the court in which such charge is pending, whichever date last occurs. If a defendant consents in writing to be tried before a magistrate [United States magistrate judge] on a complaint, the trial shall commence within seventy days from the date of such consent.

(2) Unless the defendant consents in writing to the contrary, the trial shall not commence less than thirty days from the date on which the defendant first appears through counsel or expressly waives counsel and elects to proceed pro se.

(d) (1) If any indictment or information is dismissed upon motion of the defendant, or any charge contained in a complaint filed against an individual is dismissed or otherwise dropped, and thereafter a complaint is filed against such defendant or individual charging him with the same offense or an offense based on the same conduct or arising from the same criminal episode, or an information or indictment is filed charging such defendant with the same offense or an offense based on the same conduct or arising from the same criminal episode, the provisions of subsections (b) and (c) of this section shall be applicable with respect to such subsequent complaint, indictment, or information, as the case may be.

(2) If the defendant is to be tried upon an indictment or information dismissed by a trial court and reinstated following an appeal, the trial shall commence within seventy days from the date the action occasioning the trial becomes final, except that the court retrying the case may extend the period for trial not to exceed one hundred and eighty days from the date the action occasioning the trial becomes final if the unavailability of witnesses or other factors resulting from the passage of time shall make trial within seventy days impractical. The periods of delay enumerated in section 3161(h) are excluded in computing the time limitations specified in this section. The sanctions of section 3162 apply to this subsection.

(e) If the defendant is to be tried again following a declaration by the trial judge of a mistrial or following an order of such judge for a new trial, the trial shall commence within seventy days from the date the action occasioning the retrial becomes final. If the defendant is to be tried again following an appeal or a collateral attack, the trial shall commence within seventy days from the date the action occasioning the retrial becomes final, except that the court retrying the case may extend the period for retrial not to exceed one hundred and eighty days from the date the action occasioning the retrial becomes final if unavailability of witnesses or other factors resulting from passage of time shall make trial within seventy days impractical. The periods of delay enumerated in section 3161(h) are excluded in computing the time limitations specified in this section. The sanctions of section 3162 apply to this subsection.

(f) Notwithstanding the provisions of subsection (b) of this section, for the first twelve-calendar-month period following the effective date of this section as set forth in section 3163(a) of this chapter[,] the time limit imposed with respect to the period between arrest and indictment by subsection (b) of this section shall be sixty days, for the second such twelve-month period such time limit shall be forty-five days and for the third such period such time limit shall be thirty-five days.

(g) Notwithstanding the provisions of subsection (c) of this section, for the first twelve-calendar-month period following the effective date of this section as set forth in section 3163(b) of this chapter, the time limit with respect to the period between arraignment and trial imposed by subsection (c) of this section shall be one hundred and eighty days, for the second such twelve-month period such time limit shall be one hundred and twenty days, and for the third such period such time limit with respect to the period between arraignment and trial shall be eighty days.

(h) The following periods of delay shall be excluded in computing the time within which an information or an indictment must be filed, or in computing the time within which the trial of any such offense must commence:

(1) Any period of delay resulting from other proceedings concerning the defendant, including but not limited to—

(A) delay resulting from any proceeding, including any examinations, to determine the mental competency or physical capacity of the defendant;

(B) delay resulting from trial with respect to other charges against the defendant;

(C) delay resulting from any interlocutory appeal;

(D) delay resulting from any pretrial motion, from the filing of the motion through the conclusion of the hearing on, or other prompt disposition of, such motion;

(E) delay resulting from any proceeding relating to the transfer of a case or the removal of any defendant from another district under the Federal Rules of Criminal Procedure;

(F) delay resulting from transportation of any defendant from another district, or to and from places of examination or hospitalization, except that any time consumed in excess of ten days from the date an order of removal or an order directing such transportation, and the defendant's arrival at the destination shall be presumed to be unreasonable;

(G) delay resulting from consideration by the court of a proposed plea agreement to be entered into by the defendant and the attorney for the Government; and

(H) delay reasonably attributable to any period, not to exceed thirty days, during which any proceeding concerning the defendant is actually under advisement by the court.

(2) Any period of delay during which prosecution is deferred by the attorney for the Government pursuant to written agreement with the defendant, with the approval of the court, for the purpose of allowing the defendant to demonstrate his good conduct.

(3)(A) Any period of delay resulting from the absence or unavailability of the defendant or an essential witness.

(B) For purposes of subparagraph (A) of this paragraph, a defendant or an essential witness shall be considered absent when his whereabouts are unknown and, in addition, he is attempting to avoid apprehension or prosecution or his whereabouts cannot be determined by due diligence. For purposes of such subparagraph, a defendant or an essential witness shall be considered unavailable whenever his whereabouts are known but his presence for trial cannot be obtained by due diligence or he resists appearing at or being returned for trial.

(4) Any period of delay resulting from the fact that the defendant is mentally incompetent or physically unable to stand trial.

(5) If the information or indictment is dismissed upon motion of the attorney for the Government and thereafter a charge is filed against the defendant for the same offense, or any offense required to be joined with that offense, any period of delay from the date the charge was dismissed to the date the time limitation would commence to run as to the subsequent charge had there been no previous charge.

(6) A reasonable period of delay when the defendant is joined for trial with a codefendant as to whom the time for trial has not run and no motion for severance has been granted.

(7)(A) Any period of delay resulting from a continuance granted by any judge on his own motion or at the request of the defendant or his counsel or at the request of the attorney for the Government, if the judge granted such continuance on the basis of his findings that the ends of justice served by taking such action outweigh the best interest of the public and the defendant in a speedy trial. No such period of delay resulting from a continuance granted by the court in accordance with this paragraph shall be excludable under this subsection unless the court sets forth, in the record of the case, either orally or in writing, its reasons for finding that the ends of justice served by the granting of such continuance outweigh the best interests of the public and the defendant in a speedy trial.

(B) The factors, among others, which a judge shall consider in determining whether to grant a continuance under subparagraph (A) of this paragraph in any case are as follows:

(i) Whether the failure to grant such a continuance in the proceeding would be likely to make a continuation of such proceeding impossible, or result in a miscarriage of justice.

(ii) Whether the case is so unusual or so complex, due to the number of defendants, the nature of the prosecution, or the existence of novel questions of fact or law, that it is unreasonable to expect adequate preparation for pretrial proceedings or for the trial itself within the time limits established by this section.

(iii) Whether, in a case in which arrest precedes indictment, delay in the filing of the indictment is caused because the arrest occurs at a time such that it is unreasonable to expect return and filing of the indictment within the period specified in section 3161(b) or because the facts upon which the grand jury must base its determination are unusual or complex.

(iv) Whether the failure to grant such a continuance in a case that, taken as a whole, is not so unusual or so complex as to fall within clause (ii), would deny the defendant reasonable time to obtain counsel, would unreasonably deny the defendant or the Government continuity of counsel, or would deny counsel for the defendant or the attorney for the Government the reasonable time necessary for effective preparation, taking into account the exercise of due diligence.

(C) No continuance under subparagraph (A) of this paragraph shall be granted because of general congestion of the court's calendar, or lack of diligent preparation or failure to obtain available witnesses on the part of the attorney for the Government.

(8) Any period of delay, not to exceed one year, ordered by a district court upon an application of a party and a finding by a preponderance of the evidence that an official request, as defined in section 3292 of this title, has been made for evidence of any such offense and that it reasonably appears, or reasonably appeared at the time the request was made, that such evidence is, or was, in such foreign country.

(i) If trial did not commence within the time limitation specified in section 3161 because the defendant had entered a plea of guilty or nolo contendere subsequently withdrawn to any or all charges in an indictment or information, the defendant shall be deemed indicted with respect to all charges therein contained within the meaning of section 3161 on the day the order permitting withdrawal of the plea becomes final.

(j)(1) If the attorney for the Government knows that a person charged with an offense is serving a term of imprisonment in any penal institution, he shall promptly—

(A) undertake to obtain the presence of the prisoner for trial; or

(B) cause a detainer to be filed with the person having custody of the prisoner and request him to so advise the prisoner and to advise the prisoner of his right to demand trial.

(2) If the person having custody of such prisoner receives a
detainer, he shall promptly advise the prisoner of the charge and of
the prisoner's right to demand trial. If at any time thereafter the prisoner informs the person having custody that he does demand trial,
such person shall cause notice to that effect to be sent promptly to
the attorney for the Government who caused the detainer to be filed.

(3) Upon receipt of such notice, the attorney for the Government
shall promptly seek to obtain the presence of the prisoner for trial.

(4) When the person having custody of the prisoner receives
from the attorney for the Government a properly supported request
for temporary custody of such prisoner for trial, the prisoner shall
be made available to that attorney for the Government (subject, in
cases of interjurisdictional transfer, to any right of the prisoner to
contest the legality of his delivery).

(k)(1) If the defendant is absent (as defined by subsection (h)
(3)) on the day set for trial, and the defendant's subsequent appearance
before the court on a bench warrant or other process or surrender to
the court occurs more than twenty-one days after the day set for trial,
the defendant shall be deemed to have first appeared before a judicial
officer of the court in which the information or indictment is pending
within the meaning of subsection (c) on the date of the defendant's
subsequent appearance before the court.

(2) If the defendant is absent (as defined by subsection (h)(3))
on the day set for trial, and the defendant's subsequent appearance
before the court on a bench warrant or other process or surrender
to the court occurs not more than twenty-one days after the day set
for trial, the time limit required by subsection (c), as extended by
subsection (h), shall be further extended by twenty-one days.

18 U.S.C. §3162. Sanctions

(a)(1) If, in the case of any individual against whom a complaint is
filed charging such individual with an offense, no indictment or information is filed within the time limit required by section 3161(b) as
extended by section 3161(h) of this chapter, such charge against that
individual contained in such complaint shall be dismissed or otherwise
dropped. In determining whether to dismiss the case with or without
prejudice, the court shall consider, among others, each of the following
factors: the seriousness of the offense; the facts and circumstances of

the case which led to the dismissal; and the impact of a reprosecution on the administration of this chapter [18 U.S.C. §§ 3161 et seq.] and on the administration of justice.

(2) If a defendant is not brought to trial within the time limit required by section 3161(c) as extended by section 3161(h), the information or indictment shall be dismissed on motion of the defendant. The defendant shall have the burden of proof of supporting such motion but the Government shall have the burden of going forward with the evidence in connection with any exclusion of time under subparagraph 3161(h)(3).

In determining whether to dismiss the case with or without prejudice, the court shall consider, among others, each of the following factors: the seriousness of the offense; the facts and circumstances of the case which led to the dismissal; and the impact of a reprosecution on the administration of this chapter [18 U.S.C. §§ 3161 et seq.] and on the administration of justice. Failure of the defendant to move for dismissal prior to trial or entry of a plea of guilty or nolo contendere shall constitute a waiver of the right to dismissal under this section.

(b) In any case in which counsel for the defendant or the attorney for the Government

(1) knowingly allows the case to be set for trial without disclosing the fact that a necessary witness would be unavailable for trial;

(2) files a motion solely for the purpose of delay, which he knows is totally frivolous and without merit;

(3) makes a statement for the purpose of obtaining a continuance that he knows to be false and that is material to the granting of a continuance; or

(4) otherwise willfully fails to proceed to trial without justification consistent with section 3161 of this chapter, the court may punish any such counsel or attorney, as follows:

(A) in the case of an appointed defense counsel, by reducing the amount of compensation that otherwise would have been paid to such counsel pursuant to section 3006A of this title in an amount not to exceed 25 per centum thereof;

(B) in the case of a counsel retained in connection with the defense of a defendant, by imposing on such counsel a fine of not to exceed 25 per centum of the compensation to which he is entitled in connection with his defense of such defendant;

(C) by imposing on any attorney for the Government a fine of not to exceed $250;

(D) by denying any such counsel or attorney for the Government the right to practice before the court considering such case for a period of not to exceed 90 days; or

(E) by filing a report with an appropriate disciplinary committee.

The authority to punish provided for by this subsection shall be in addition to any other authority or power available to such court.

(c) The court shall follow procedures established in the Federal Rules of Criminal Procedure in punishing any counsel or attorney for the Government pursuant to this section.

18 U.S.C. §3164.   Persons Detained or Designated As Being of High Risk

(a) The trial or other disposition of cases involving—

(1) a detained person who is being held in detention solely because he is awaiting trial, and

(2) a released person who is awaiting trial and has been designated by the attorney for the Government as being of high risk, shall be accorded priority.

(b) The trial of any person described in subsection (a)(1) or (a)(2) of this section shall commence not later than ninety days following the beginning of such continuous detention or designation of high risk by the attorney for the Government. The periods of delay enumerated in section 3161(h) are excluded in computing the time limitation specified in this section.

(c) Failure to commence trial of a detainee as specified in subsection (b), through no fault of the accused or his counsel, or failure to commence trial of a designated releasee as specified in subsection (b), through no fault of the attorney for the Government, shall result in the automatic review by the court of the conditions of release. No detainee, as defined in subsection (a), shall be held in custody pending trial after the expiration of such ninety-day period required for the commencement of his trial. A designated releasee, as defined in subsection (a), who is found by the court to have intentionally delayed the trial of his case shall be subject to an order of the court modifying his nonfinancial conditions of release under this title to insure that he shall appear at trial as required.

18 U.S.C. §3173. Sixth Amendment Rights

No provision of this chapter [18 U.S.C. §§ 3161 et seq.] shall be interpreted as a bar to any claim of denial of speedy trial as required by amendment VI of the Constitution.

Jencks Act

18 U.S.C. §3500. Demands for Production of Statements and Reports of Witnesses

(a) In any criminal prosecution brought by the United States, no statement or report in the possession of the United States which was made by a Government witness or prospective Government witness (other than the defendant) shall be the subject of subpoena, discovery, or inspection until said witness has testified on direct examination in the trial of the case.

(b) After a witness called by the United States has testified on direct examination, the court shall, on motion of the defendant, order the United States to produce any statement (as hereinafter defined) of the witness in the possession of the United States which relates to the subject matter as to which the witness has testified. If the entire contents of any such statement relate to the subject matter of the testimony of the witness, the court shall order it to be delivered directly to the defendant for his examination and use.

(c) If the United States claims that any statement ordered to be produced under this section contains matter which does not relate to the subject matter of the testimony of the witness, the court shall order the United States to deliver such statement for the inspection of the court in camera. Upon such delivery the court shall excise the portions of such statement which do not relate to the subject matter of the testimony of the witness. With such material excised, the court shall then direct delivery of such statement to the defendant for his use. If, pursuant to such procedure, any portion of such statement is withheld from the defendant and the defendant objects to such withholding, and the trial is continued to an adjudication of the guilt of the defendant, the entire text of such statement shall be preserved by the United States and, in the event the defendant appeals, shall be made available to the appellate court for the purpose of determining the correctness of the ruling of the trial judge. Whenever any statement is delivered to a defendant pursuant to this section, the court in its discretion, upon application of said defendant, may recess proceedings in the trial for such time as it may determine to be reasonably required for the examination of such statement by said defendant and his preparation for its use in the trial.

(d) If the United States elects not to comply with an order of the court under subsection (b) or (c) hereof to deliver to the defendant any such statement, or such portion thereof as the court may direct, the court shall strike from the record the testimony of the witness, and the trial shall proceed unless the court in its discretion shall determine that the interests of justice require that a mistrial be declared.

(e) The term "statement," as used in subsections (b), (c), and (d) of this section in relation to any witness called by the United States, means—

(1) a written statement made by said witness and signed or otherwise adopted or approved by him;

(2) a stenographic, mechanical, electrical, or other recording, or a transcription thereof, which is a substantially verbatim recital of an oral statement made by said witness and recorded contemporaneously with the making of such oral statement; or

(3) a statement, however taken or recorded, or a transcription thereof, if any, made by said witness to a grand jury.

Criminal Appeals Act of 1970 (as amended)

18 U.S.C. §3731. Appeal by United States

In a criminal case an appeal by the United States shall lie to a court of appeals from a decision, judgment, or order of a district court dismissing an indictment or information or granting a new trial after verdict or judgment, as to any one or more counts, or any part thereof, except that no appeal shall lie where the double jeopardy clause of the United States Constitution prohibits further prosecution.

An appeal by the United States shall lie to a court of appeals from a decision or order of a district court suppressing or excluding evidence or requiring the return of seized property in a criminal proceeding, not made after the defendant has been put in jeopardy and before the verdict or finding on an indictment or information, if the United States attorney certifies to the district court that the appeal is not taken for purpose of delay and that the evidence is a substantial proof of a fact material in the proceeding.

An appeal by the United States shall lie to a court of appeals from a decision or order, entered by a district court of the United States, granting the release of a person charged with or convicted of an offense, or denying a motion for revocation of, or modification of the conditions of, a decision or order granting release.

The appeal in all such cases shall be taken within thirty days after the decision, judgment, or order has been rendered and shall be diligently prosecuted.

The provisions of this section shall be liberally construed to effectuate its purposes.

Crime Victims' Rights Act

18 U.S.C. §3771.   Crime Victims' Rights

(a) Rights of crime victims.—A crime victim has the following rights:

(1) The right to be reasonably protected from the accused.

(2) The right to reasonable, accurate, and timely notice of any public court proceeding, or any parole proceeding, involving the crime or of any release or escape of the accused.

(3) The right not to be excluded from any such public court proceeding, unless the court, after receiving clear and convincing evidence, determines that testimony by the victim would be materially altered if the victim heard other testimony at that proceeding.

(4) The right to be reasonably heard at any public proceeding in the district court involving release, plea, sentencing, or any parole proceeding.

(5) The reasonable right to confer with the attorney for the Government in the case.

(6) The right to full and timely restitution as provided in law.

(7) The right to proceedings free from unreasonable delay.

(8) The right to be treated with fairness and with respect for the victim's dignity and privacy.

(9) The right to be informed in a timely manner of any plea bargain or deferred prosecution agreement.

(10) The right to be informed of the rights under this section and the services described in section 503(c) of the Victims' Rights and Restitution Act of 1990 (42 U.S.C. 10607(c)) and provided contact information for the Office of the Victims' Rights Ombudsman of the Department of Justice.

(b) Rights afforded.—

(1) In general.—In any court proceeding involving an offense against a crime victim, the court shall ensure that the crime victim is afforded the rights described in subsection (a). Before making a determination described in subsection (a)(3), the court shall make every effort to permit the fullest attendance possible by the victim and shall consider reasonable alternatives to the exclusion of the victim from the criminal proceeding. The reasons for any decision denying relief under this chapter shall be clearly stated on the record.

(2) Habeas corpus proceedings.—

(A) In general.—In a Federal habeas corpus proceeding arising out of a State conviction, the court shall ensure that a crime victim is afforded the rights described in paragraphs (3), (4), (7), and (8) of subsection (a).

(B) Enforcement.—

(i) In general.—These rights may be enforced by the crime victim or the crime victim's lawful representative in the manner described in paragraphs (1) and (3) of subsection (d).

(ii) Multiple victims.—In a case involving multiple victims, subsection (d)(2) shall also apply.

(C) Limitation.—This paragraph relates to the duties of a court in relation to the rights of a crime victim in Federal habeas corpus proceedings arising out of a State conviction, and does not give rise to any obligation or requirement applicable to personnel of any agency of the Executive Branch of the Federal Government.

(D) Definition.—For purposes of this paragraph, the term "crime victim" means the person against whom the State offense is committed or, if that person is killed or incapacitated, that person's family member or other lawful representative.

(c) Best efforts to accord rights.—

(1) Government.—Officers and employees of the Department of Justice and other departments and agencies of the United States engaged in the detection, investigation, or prosecution of crime shall

make their best efforts to see that crime victims are notified of, and accorded, the rights described in subsection (a).

(2) Advice of attorney. — The prosecutor shall advise the crime victim that the crime victim can seek the advice of an attorney with respect to the rights described in subsection (a).

(3) Notice. — Notice of release otherwise required pursuant to this chapter shall not be given if such notice may endanger the safety of any person.

(d) Enforcement and limitations. —

(1) Rights. — The crime victim or the crime victim's lawful representative, and the attorney for the Government may assert the rights described in subsection (a). A person accused of the crime may not obtain any form of relief under this chapter.

(2) Multiple crime victims. — In a case where the court finds that the number of crime victims makes it impracticable to accord all of the crime victims the rights described in subsection (a), the court shall fashion a reasonable procedure to give effect to this chapter that does not unduly complicate or prolong the proceedings.

(3) Motion for relief and writ of mandamus. — The rights described in subsection (a) shall be asserted in the district court in which a defendant is being prosecuted for the crime or, if no prosecution is underway, in the district court in the district in which the crime occurred. The district court shall take up and decide any motion asserting a victim's right forthwith. If the district court denies the relief sought, the movant may petition the court of appeals for a writ of mandamus. The court of appeals may issue the writ on the order of a single judge pursuant to circuit rule or the Federal Rules of Appellate Procedure. The court of appeals shall take up and decide such application forthwith within 72 hours after the petition has been filed, unless the litigants, with the approval of the court, have stipulated to a different time period for consideration. In deciding such application, the court of appeals shall apply ordinary standards of appellate review. In no event shall proceedings be stayed or subject to a continuance of more than five days for purposes of enforcing this chapter. If the court of appeals denies the relief sought, the reasons for the denial shall be clearly stated on the record in a written opinion.

(4) Error. — In any appeal in a criminal case, the Government may assert as error the district court's denial of any crime victim's right in the proceeding to which the appeal relates.

(5) Limitation on relief.—In no case shall a failure to afford a right under this chapter provide grounds for a new trial. A victim may make a motion to re-open a plea or sentence only if—

(A) the victim has asserted the right to be heard before or during the proceeding at issue and such right was denied;

(B) the victim petitions the court of appeals for a writ of mandamus within 14 days; and

(C) in the case of a plea, the accused has not pled to the highest offense charged. This paragraph does not affect the victim's right to restitution as provided in title 18, United States Code.

(6) No cause of action.—Nothing in this chapter shall be construed to authorize a cause of action for damages or to create, to enlarge, or to imply any duty or obligation to any victim or other person for the breach of which the United States or any of its officers or employees could be held liable in damages. Nothing in this chapter shall be construed to impair the prosecutorial discretion of the Attorney General or any officer under his direction.

(e) Definitions.—For the purposes of this chapter:

(1) Court of appeals.—The term "court of appeals" means—

(A) the United States court of appeals for the judicial district in which a defendant is being prosecuted; or

(B) for a prosecution in the Superior Court of the District of Columbia, the District of Columbia Court of Appeals.

(2) Crime victim.—

(A) In general.—The term "crime victim" means a person directly and proximately harmed as a result of the commission of a Federal offense or an offense in the District of Columbia.

(B) Minors and certain other victims.—In the case of a crime victim who is under 18 years of age, incompetent, incapacitated, or deceased, the legal guardians of the crime victim or the representatives of the crime victim's estate, family members, or any other persons appointed as suitable by the court, may assume the crime victim's rights under this chapter, but in no event shall the defendant be named as such guardian or representative.

(3) District court; court.—The terms "district court" and "court" include the Superior Court of the District of Columbia.

(f) Procedures to promote compliance.—

(1) Regulations.—Not later than 1 year after the date of enactment of this chapter, the Attorney General of the United States shall promulgate regulations to enforce the rights of crime victims and

to ensure compliance by responsible officials with the obligations described in law respecting crime victims.

(2) Contents.—The regulations promulgated under paragraph (1) shall—

(A) designate an administrative authority within the Department of Justice to receive and investigate complaints relating to the provision or violation of the rights of a crime victim;

(B) require a course of training for employees and offices of the Department of Justice that fail to comply with provisions of Federal law pertaining to the treatment of crime victims, and otherwise assist such employees and offices in responding more effectively to the needs of crime victims;

(C) contain disciplinary sanctions, including suspension or termination from employment, for employees of the Department of Justice who willfully or wantonly fail to comply with provisions of Federal law pertaining to the treatment of crime victims; and

(D) provide that the Attorney General, or the designee of the Attorney General, shall be the final arbiter of the complaint, and that there shall be no judicial review of the final decision of the Attorney General by a complainant.

Habeas Corpus Act of 1867 (as amended by Antiterrorism and Effective Death Penalty Act of 1996)

28 U.S.C. §2241. Power to Grant Writ

(a) Writs of habeas corpus may be granted by the Supreme Court, any justice thereof, the district courts, and any circuit judge within their respective jurisdictions. The order of a circuit judge shall be entered in the records of the district court of the district wherein the restraint complained of is had.

(b) The Supreme Court, any justice thereof, and any circuit judge may decline to entertain an application for a writ of habeas corpus and may transfer the application for hearing and determination to the district court having jurisdiction to entertain it.

(c) The writ of habeas corpus shall not extend to a prisoner unless—

(1) He is in custody under or by color of the authority of the United States or is committed for trial before some court thereof; or

(2) He is in custody for an act done or omitted in pursuance of an Act of Congress, or an order, process, judgment or decree of a court or judge of the United States; or

(3) He is in custody in violation of the Constitution or laws or treaties of the United States; or

(4) He, being a citizen of a foreign state and domiciled therein, is in custody for an act done or omitted under any alleged right, title, authority, privilege, protection, or exemption claimed under the commission, order or sanction of any foreign state, or under color thereof, the validity and effect of which depend upon the law of nations; or

(5) It is necessary to bring him into court to testify or for trial.

(d) Where an application for a writ of habeas corpus is made by a person in custody under the judgment and sentence of a State court of a State which contains two or more Federal judicial districts, the application may be filed in the district court for the district wherein such person is in custody or in the district court for the district within which the State court was held which convicted and sentenced him and each of such district courts shall have concurrent jurisdiction to entertain the application. The district court for the district wherein such an application is filed in the exercise of its discretion and in furtherance of justice may transfer the application to the other district court for hearing and determination.

(e) [**NOTE**—This provision, which was added to the statute as part of the Detainee Treatment Act of 2005 and which purported to deny access to habeas corpus for aliens detained by the U.S. Department of Defense at Guantanamo Bay as alleged "enemy combatants," was held unconstitutional by the U.S. Supreme Court in Boumediene v. Bush, 553 U.S. 723 (2008). See the main casebook, Chapter 17, at pages 1673-1674, for further discussion of *Boumediene.*—EDS.]

28 U.S.C. §2242. Application

Application for a writ of habeas corpus shall be in writing signed and verified by the person for whose relief it is intended or by someone acting in his behalf.

It shall allege the facts concerning the applicant's commitment or detention, the name of the person who has custody over him and by virtue of what claim or authority, if known.

It may be amended or supplemented as provided in the rules of procedure applicable to civil actions.

If addressed to the Supreme Court, a justice thereof, or a circuit judge, it shall state the reasons for not making application to the district court of the district in which the applicant is held.

28 U.S.C. §2243. Issuance of Writ; Return; Hearing; Decision

A court, justice, or judge entertaining an application for a writ of habeas corpus shall forthwith award the writ or issue an order directing the respondent to show cause why the writ should not be granted, unless it appears from the application that the applicant or person detained is not entitled thereto.

The writ, or order to show cause, shall be directed to the person having custody of the person detained. It shall be returned within three days unless for good cause additional time, not exceeding twenty days, is allowed.

The person to whom the writ or order is directed shall make a return certifying the true cause of the detention.

When the writ or order is returned a day shall be set for hearing, not more than five days after the return unless for good cause additional time is allowed.

Unless the application for the writ and the return present only issues of law, the person to whom the writ is directed shall be required to produce at the hearing the body of the person detained.

The applicant or the person detained may, under oath, deny any of the facts set forth in the return or allege any other material facts.

The return and all suggestions made against it may be amended, by leave of court, before or after being filed.

The court shall summarily hear and determine the facts and dispose of the matter as law and justice require.

28 U.S.C. §2244. Finality of Determination

(a) No circuit or district judge shall be required to entertain an application for a writ of habeas corpus to inquire into the detention of a person pursuant to a judgment of a court of the United States if it appears that the legality of such detention has been determined by a judge or court of the United States on a prior application for a writ of habeas corpus, except as provided in section 2255.

(b)(1) A claim presented in a second or successive habeas corpus application under section 2254 that was presented in a prior application shall be dismissed.

(2) A claim presented in a second or successive habeas corpus application under section 2254 that was not presented in a prior application shall be dismissed unless—

(A) the applicant shows that the claim relies on a new rule of constitutional law, made retroactive to cases on collateral review by the Supreme Court, that was previously unavailable; or

(B)(i) the factual predicate for the claim could not have been discovered previously through the exercise of due diligence; and

(ii) the facts underlying the claim, if proven and viewed in light of the evidence as a whole, would be sufficient to establish by clear and convincing evidence that, but for constitutional error, no reasonable factfinder would have found the applicant guilty of the underlying offense.

(3)(A) Before a second or successive application permitted by this section is filed in the district court, the applicant shall move in the appropriate court of appeals for an order authorizing the district court to consider the application.

(B) A motion in the court of appeals for an order authorizing the district court to consider a second or successive application shall be determined by a three-judge panel of the court of appeals.

(C) The court of appeals may authorize the filing of a second or successive application only if it determines that the application makes a prima facie showing that the application satisfies the requirements of this subsection.

(D) The court of appeals shall grant or deny the authorization to file a second or successive application not later than 30 days after the filing of the motion.

(E) The grant or denial of an authorization by a court of appeals to file a second or successive application shall not be appealable and shall not be the subject of a petition for rehearing or for a writ of certiorari.

(4) A district court shall dismiss any claim presented in a second or successive application that the court of appeals has authorized to be filed unless the applicant shows that the claim satisfies the requirements of this section.

(c) In a habeas corpus proceeding brought in behalf of a person in custody pursuant to the judgment of a State court, a prior judgment of the Supreme Court of the United States on an appeal or review by a writ of certiorari at the instance of the prisoner of the decision of such State court, shall be conclusive as to all issues of fact or law with respect to an asserted denial of a Federal right which constitutes ground for discharge in a habeas corpus proceeding, actually adjudicated by the Supreme Court therein, unless the applicant for the writ of habeas corpus shall plead and the court shall find the existence of a material and controlling fact which did not appear in the record of the proceeding in the Supreme Court and the court shall further find that the applicant for the writ of habeas corpus could not have caused such fact to appear in such record by the exercise of reasonable diligence.

(d)(1) A one-year period of limitation shall apply to an application for a writ of habeas corpus by a person in custody pursuant to the judgment of a State court. The limitation period shall run from the latest of—

    (A) the date on which the judgment became final by the conclusion of direct review or the expiration of the time for seeking such review;

    (B) the date on which the impediment to filing an application created by State action in violation of the Constitution or laws of the United States is removed, if the applicant was prevented from filing by such State action;

    (C) the date on which the constitutional right asserted was initially recognized by the Supreme Court, if the right has been newly recognized by the Supreme Court and made retroactively applicable to cases on collateral review; or

    (D) the date on which the factual predicate of the claim or claims presented could have been discovered through the exercise of due diligence.

(2) The time during which a properly filed application for State post-conviction or other collateral review with respect to the pertinent judgment or claim is pending shall not be counted toward any period of limitation under this subsection.

28 U.S.C. §2253. Appeal

(a) In a habeas corpus proceeding or a proceeding under section 2255 before a district judge, the final order shall be subject to review, on appeal, by the court of appeals for the circuit in which the proceeding is held.

(b) There shall be no right of appeal from a final order in a proceeding to test the validity of a warrant to remove to another district or place for commitment or trial a person charged with a criminal offense against the United States, or to test the validity of such person's detention pending removal proceedings.

(c)(1) Unless a circuit justice or judge issues a certificate of appealability, an appeal may not be taken to the court of appeals from—

(A) the final order in a habeas corpus proceeding in which the detention complained of arises out of process issued by a State court; or

(B) the final order in a proceeding under section 2255.

(2) A certificate of appealability may issue under paragraph (1) only if the applicant has made a substantial showing of the denial of a constitutional right.

(3) The certificate of appealability under paragraph (1) shall indicate which specific issue or issues satisfy the showing required by paragraph (2).

28 U.S.C. §2254. State Custody; Remedies in Federal Courts

(a) The Supreme Court, a Justice thereof, a circuit judge, or a district court shall entertain an application for a writ of habeas corpus in behalf of a person in custody pursuant to the judgment of a State court only on the ground that he is in custody in violation of the Constitution or laws or treaties of the United States.

(b)(1) An application for a writ of habeas corpus on behalf of a person in custody pursuant to the judgment of a State court shall not be granted unless it appears that—

(A) the applicant has exhausted the remedies available in the courts of the State; or

(B) (i) there is an absence of available State corrective process; or

(ii) circumstances exist that render such process ineffective to protect the rights of the applicant.

(2) An application for a writ of habeas corpus may be denied on the merits, notwithstanding the failure of the applicant to exhaust the remedies available in the courts of the State.

(3) A State shall not be deemed to have waived the exhaustion requirement or be estopped from reliance upon the requirement unless the State, through counsel, expressly waives the requirement.

(c) An applicant shall not be deemed to have exhausted the remedies available in the courts of the State, within the meaning of this section, if he has the right under the law of the State to raise, by any available procedure, the question presented.

(d) An application for a writ of habeas corpus on behalf of a person in custody pursuant to the judgment of a State court shall not be granted with respect to any claim that was adjudicated on the merits in State court proceedings unless the adjudication of the claim—

(1) resulted in a decision that was contrary to, or involved an unreasonable application of, clearly established Federal law, as determined by the Supreme Court of the United States; or

(2) resulted in a decision that was based on an unreasonable determination of the facts in light of the evidence presented in the State court proceeding.

(e)(1) In a proceeding instituted by an application for a writ of habeas corpus by a person in custody pursuant to the judgment of a State court, a determination of a factual issue made by a State court shall be presumed to be correct. The applicant shall have the burden of rebutting the presumption of correctness by clear and convincing evidence.

(2) If the applicant has failed to develop the factual basis of a claim in State court proceedings, the court shall not hold an evidentiary hearing on the claim unless the applicant shows that—

(A) the claim relies on—

(i) a new rule of constitutional law, made retroactive to cases on collateral review by the Supreme Court, that was previously unavailable; or

(ii) a factual predicate that could not have been previously discovered through the exercise of due diligence; and

(B) the facts underlying the claim would be sufficient to establish by clear and convincing evidence that but for constitutional error, no reasonable factfinder would have found the applicant guilty of the underlying offense.

(f) If the applicant challenges the sufficiency of the evidence adduced in such State court proceeding to support the State court's determination of a factual issue made therein, the applicant, if able, shall produce that part of the record pertinent to a determination of the sufficiency of the evidence to support such determination. If the applicant, because of indigency or other reason is unable to produce such part of the record, then the State shall produce such part of the record and the Federal court shall direct the State to do so by order directed to an appropriate State official. If the State cannot provide such pertinent part of the record, then the court shall determine under the existing facts and circumstances what weight shall be given to the State court's factual determination.

(g) A copy of the official records of the State court, duly certified by the clerk of such court to be a true and correct copy of a finding, judicial opinion, or other reliable written indicia showing such a factual determination by the State court shall be admissible in the Federal court proceeding.

(h) Except as provided in section 408 of the Controlled Substance Acts [21 U.S.C. § 848], in all proceedings brought under this section, and any subsequent proceedings on review, the court may appoint counsel for an applicant who is or becomes financially unable to afford counsel, except as provided by a rule promulgated by the Supreme Court pursuant to statutory authority. Appointment of counsel under this section shall be governed by section 3006A of title 18.

(i) The ineffectiveness or incompetence of counsel during Federal or State collateral post-conviction proceedings shall not be a ground for relief in a proceeding arising under section 2254.

Collateral Review for Federal Prisoners

28 U.S.C. §2255. Federal Custody; Remedies on Motion Attacking Sentence

(a) A prisoner in custody under sentence of a court established by Act of Congress claiming the right to be released upon the ground that the sentence was imposed in violation of the Constitution or laws of the United States, or that the court was without jurisdiction to impose such sentence, or that the sentence was in excess of the maximum authorized by law, or is otherwise subject to collateral attack, may move the court which imposed the sentence to vacate, set aside or correct the sentence.

(b) Unless the motion and the files and records of the case conclusively show that the prisoner is entitled to no relief, the court shall cause notice thereof to be served upon the United States attorney, grant a prompt hearing thereon, determine the issues and make findings of fact and conclusions of law with respect thereto. If the court finds that the judgment was rendered without jurisdiction, or that the sentence imposed was not authorized by law or otherwise open to collateral attack, or that there has been such a denial or infringement of the constitutional rights of the prisoner as to render the judgment vulnerable to collateral attack, the court shall vacate and set the judgment aside and shall discharge the prisoner or resentence him or grant a new trial or correct the sentence as may appear appropriate.

(c) A court may entertain and determine such motion without requiring the production of the prisoner at the hearing.

(d) An appeal may be taken to the court of appeals from the order entered on the motion as from the final judgment on application for a writ of habeas corpus.

(e) An application for a writ of habeas corpus in behalf of a prisoner who is authorized to apply for relief by motion pursuant to this section, shall not be entertained if it appears that the applicant has failed to apply for relief, by motion, to the court which sentenced him, or that such court has denied him relief, unless it also appears that the remedy by motion is inadequate or ineffective to test the legality of his detention.

(f) A one-year period of limitation shall apply to a motion under this section. The limitation period shall run from the latest of—

(1) the date on which the judgment of conviction becomes final;

(2) the date on which the impediment to making a motion created by governmental action in violation of the Constitution or laws of the United States is removed, if the movant was prevented from making a motion by such governmental action;

(3) the date on which the right asserted was initially recognized by the Supreme Court, if that right has been newly recognized by the Supreme Court and made retroactively applicable to cases on collateral review; or

(4) the date on which the facts supporting the claim or claims presented could have been discovered through the exercise of due diligence.

(g) Except as provided in section 408 of the Controlled Substances Act [21 U.S.C. § 848], in all proceedings brought under this section, and any subsequent proceedings on review, the court may appoint counsel, except as provided by a rule promulgated by the Supreme Court pursuant to statutory authority. Appointment of counsel under this section shall be governed by section 3006A of title 18.

(h) A second or successive motion must be certified as provided in section 2244 by a panel of the appropriate court of appeals to contain—

(1) newly discovered evidence that, if proven and viewed in light of the evidence as a whole, would be sufficient to establish by clear and convincing evidence that no reasonable factfinder would have found the movant guilty of the offense; or

(2) a new rule of constitutional law, made retroactive to cases on collateral review by the Supreme Court, that was previously unavailable.

Foreign Intelligence Surveillance Act

50 U.S.C. § 1801.   Definitions

As used in this subchapter:

(a) "Foreign power" means—

(1) a foreign government or any component thereof, whether or not recognized by the United States;

(2) a faction of a foreign nation or nations, not substantially composed of United States persons;

(3) an entity that is openly acknowledged by a foreign government or governments to be directed and controlled by such foreign government or governments;

(4) a group engaged in international terrorism or activities in preparation therefor;

(5) a foreign-based political organization, not substantially composed of United States persons;

(6) an entity that is directed and controlled by a foreign government or governments; or

(7) an entity not substantially composed of United States persons that is engaged in the international proliferation of weapons of mass destruction.

(b) "Agent of a foreign power" means—

(1) any person other than a United States person, who—

(A) acts in the United States as an officer or employee of a foreign power, or as a member of a foreign power as defined in subsection (a)(4), irrespective of whether the person is inside the United States;

(B) acts for or on behalf of a foreign power which engages in clandestine intelligence activities in the United States contrary to the interests of the United States, when the circumstances indicate that such person may engage in such activities, or when such person knowingly aids or abets any person in the conduct of such activities or knowingly conspires with any person to engage in such activities;

(C) Omitted

(D) engages in the international proliferation of weapons of mass destruction, or activities in preparation therefor; or

(E) engages in the international proliferation of weapons of mass destruction, or activities in preparation therefor, for or on behalf of a foreign power, or knowingly aids or abets any person in the conduct of such proliferation or activities in preparation therefor, or knowingly conspires with any person to engage in such proliferation or activities in preparation therefor; or

(2) any person who—

(A) knowingly engages in clandestine intelligence gathering activities for or on behalf of a foreign power, which activities involve or may involve a violation of the criminal statutes of the United States;

(B) pursuant to the direction of an intelligence service or network of a foreign power, knowingly engages in any other clandestine intelligence activities for or on behalf of such foreign power, which activities involve or are about to involve a violation of the criminal statutes of the United States;

(C) knowingly engages in sabotage or international terrorism, or activities that are in preparation therefor, for or on behalf of a foreign power;

(D) knowingly enters the United States under a false or fraudulent identity for or on behalf of a foreign power or, while in the United States, knowingly assumes a false or fraudulent identity for or on behalf of a foreign power; or

(E) knowingly aids or abets any person in the conduct of activities described in subparagraph (A), (B), or (C) or knowingly conspires with any person to engage in activities described in subparagraph (A), (B), or (C).

(c) "International terrorism" means activities that—

(1) involve violent acts or acts dangerous to human life that are a violation of the criminal laws of the United States or of any

State, or that would be a criminal violation if committed within the jurisdiction of the United States or any State;

    (2) appear to be intended—

        (A) to intimidate or coerce a civilian population;

        (B) to influence the policy of a government by intimidation or coercion; or

        (C) to affect the conduct of a government by assassination or kidnapping; and

    (3) occur totally outside the United States, or transcend national boundaries in terms of the means by which they are accomplished, the persons they appear intended to coerce or intimidate, or the locale in which their perpetrators operate or seek asylum.

    (d) "Sabotage" means activities that involve a violation of chapter 105 of Title 18, or that would involve such a violation if committed against the United States.

    (e) "Foreign intelligence information" means—

    (1) information that relates to, and if concerning a United States person is necessary to, the ability of the United States to protect against—

        (A) actual or potential attack or other grave hostile acts of a foreign power or an agent of a foreign power;

        (B) sabotage, international terrorism, or the international proliferation of weapons of mass destruction by a foreign power or an agent of a foreign power; or

        (C) clandestine intelligence activities by an intelligence service or network of a foreign power or by an agent of a foreign power; or

    (2) information with respect to a foreign power or foreign territory that relates to, and if concerning a United States person is necessary to—

        (A) the national defense or the security of the United States; or

        (B) the conduct of the foreign affairs of the United States.

    (f) "Electronic surveillance" means—

    (1) the acquisition by an electronic, mechanical, or other surveillance device of the contents of any wire or radio communication sent by or intended to be received by a particular, known United States person who is in the United States, if the contents are acquired by intentionally targeting that United States person, under circumstances in which a person has a reasonable expectation of privacy and a warrant would be required for law enforcement purposes;

(2) the acquisition by an electronic, mechanical, or other surveillance device of the contents of any wire communication to or from a person in the United States, without the consent of any party thereto, if such acquisition occurs in the United States, but does not include the acquisition of those communications of computer trespassers that would be permissible under section 2511(2)(i) of Title 18;

(3) the intentional acquisition by an electronic, mechanical, or other surveillance device of the contents of any radio communication, under circumstances in which a person has a reasonable expectation of privacy and a warrant would be required for law enforcement purposes, and if both the sender and all intended recipients are located within the United States; or

(4) the installation or use of an electronic, mechanical, or other surveillance device in the United States for monitoring to acquire information, other than from a wire or radio communication, under circumstances in which a person has a reasonable expectation of privacy and a warrant would be required for law enforcement purposes.

(g) "Attorney General" means the Attorney General of the United States (or Acting Attorney General), the Deputy Attorney General, or, upon the designation of the Attorney General, the Assistant Attorney General designated as the Assistant Attorney General for National Security under section 507A of title 28.

(h) "Minimization procedures", with respect to electronic surveillance, means—

(1) specific procedures, which shall be adopted by the Attorney General, that are reasonably designed in light of the purpose and technique of the particular surveillance, to minimize the acquisition and retention, and prohibit the dissemination, of nonpublicly available information concerning unconsenting United States persons consistent with the need of the United States to obtain, produce, and disseminate foreign intelligence information;

(2) procedures that require that nonpublicly available information, which is not foreign intelligence information, as defined in subsection (e)(1), shall not be disseminated in a manner that identifies any United States person, without such person's consent, unless such person's identity is necessary to understand foreign intelligence information or assess its importance;

(3) notwithstanding paragraphs (1) and (2), procedures that allow for the retention and dissemination of information that is evidence of a crime which has been, is being, or is about to be

committed and that is to be retained or disseminated for law enforcement purposes; and

(4) notwithstanding paragraphs (1), (2), and (3), with respect to any electronic surveillance approved pursuant to section 1802(a) of this title, procedures that require that no contents of any communication to which a United States person is a party shall be disclosed, disseminated, or used for any purpose or retained for longer than 72 hours unless a court order under section 1805 of this title is obtained or unless the Attorney General determines that the information indicates a threat of death or serious bodily harm to any person.

(i) "United States person" means a citizen of the United States, an alien lawfully admitted for permanent residence (as defined in section 1101(a)(20) of Title 8), an unincorporated association a substantial number of members of which are citizens of the United States or aliens lawfully admitted for permanent residence, or a corporation which is incorporated in the United States, but does not include a corporation or an association which is a foreign power, as defined in subsection (a)(1), (2), or (3).

(j) "United States", when used in a geographic sense, means all areas under the territorial sovereignty of the United States and the Trust Territory of the Pacific Islands.

(k) "Aggrieved person" means a person who is the target of an electronic surveillance or any other person whose communications or activities were subject to electronic surveillance.

(l) "Wire communication" means any communication while it is being carried by a wire, cable, or other like connection furnished or operated by any person engaged as a common carrier in providing or operating such facilities for the transmission of interstate or foreign communications.

(m) "Person" means any individual, including any officer or employee of the Federal Government, or any group, entity, association, corporation, or foreign power.

(n) "Contents", when used with respect to a communication, includes any information concerning the identity of the parties to such communication or the existence, substance, purport, or meaning of that communication.

(o) "State" means any State of the United States, the District of Columbia, the Commonwealth of Puerto Rico, the Trust Territory of the Pacific Islands, and any territory or possession of the United States.

(p) "Weapon of mass destruction" means—

(1) any explosive, incendiary, or poison gas device that is designed, intended, or has the capability to cause a mass casualty incident;

(2) any weapon that is designed, intended, or has the capability to cause death or serious bodily injury to a significant number of persons through the release, dissemination, or impact of toxic or poisonous chemicals or their precursors;

(3) any weapon involving a biological agent, toxin, or vector (as such terms are defined in section 178 of Title 18) that is designed, intended, or has the capability to cause death, illness, or serious bodily injury to a significant number of persons; or

(4) any weapon that is designed, intended, or has the capability to release radiation or radioactivity causing death, illness, or serious bodily injury to a significant number of persons.

50 U.S.C. §1802. Electronic surveillance authorization without court order; certification by Attorney General; reports to Congressional committees; transmittal under seal; duties and compensation of communication common carrier; applications; jurisdiction of court

(a)(1) Notwithstanding any other law, the President, through the Attorney General, may authorize electronic surveillance without a court order under this subchapter to acquire foreign intelligence information for periods of up to one year if the Attorney General certifies in writing under oath that—

(A) the electronic surveillance is solely directed at—

(i) the acquisition of the contents of communications transmitted by means of communications used exclusively between or among foreign powers, as defined in section 1801(a)(1), (2), or (3) of this title; or

(ii) the acquisition of technical intelligence, other than the spoken communications of individuals, from property or premises under the open and exclusive control of a foreign power, as defined in section 1801(a)(1), (2), or (3) of this title;

(B) there is no substantial likelihood that the surveillance will acquire the contents of any communication to which a United States person is a party; and

(C) the proposed minimization procedures with respect to such surveillance meet the definition of minimization procedures under section 1801(h) of this title; and if the Attorney General reports such minimization procedures and any changes thereto to the House Permanent Select Committee on Intelligence and the Senate Select Committee on Intelligence at least thirty days prior to their effective date, unless the Attorney General determines immediate action is required and notifies the committees immediately of such minimization procedures and the reason for their becoming effective immediately.

(2) An electronic surveillance authorized by this subsection may be conducted only in accordance with the Attorney General's certification and the minimization procedures adopted by him. The Attorney General shall assess compliance with such procedures and shall report such assessments to the House Permanent Select Committee on Intelligence and the Senate Select Committee on Intelligence under the provisions of section 1808(a) of this title.

(3) The Attorney General shall immediately transmit under seal to the court established under section 1803(a) of this title a copy of his certification. Such certification shall be maintained under security measures established by the Chief Justice with the concurrence of the Attorney General, in consultation with the Director of National Intelligence, and shall remain sealed unless—

(A) an application for a court order with respect to the surveillance is made under sections 1801(h)(4) and 1804 of this title; or

(B) the certification is necessary to determine the legality of the surveillance under section 1806(f) of this title.

(4) With respect to electronic surveillance authorized by this subsection, the Attorney General may direct a specified communication common carrier to—

(A) furnish all information, facilities, or technical assistance necessary to accomplish the electronic surveillance in such a manner as will protect its secrecy and produce a minimum of interference with the services that such carrier is providing its customers; and

(B) maintain under security procedures approved by the Attorney General and the Director of National Intelligence any records concerning the surveillance or the aid furnished which such carrier wishes to retain. The Government shall compensate, at the prevailing rate, such carrier for furnishing such aid.

(b) Applications for a court order under this subchapter are authorized if the President has, by written authorization, empowered the Attorney General to approve applications to the court having jurisdiction under section 1803 of this title, and a judge to whom an application is made may, notwithstanding any other law, grant an order, in conformity with section 1805 of this title, approving electronic surveillance of a foreign power or an agent of a foreign power for the purpose of obtaining foreign intelligence information, except that the court shall not have jurisdiction to grant any order approving electronic surveillance directed solely as described in paragraph (1)(A) of subsection (a) unless such surveillance may involve the acquisition of communications of any United States person.

50 U.S.C. §1862. Access to certain business records for foreign intelligence and international terrorism investigations

(a) Application for authorization

The Director of the Federal Bureau of Investigation or a designee of the Director (whose rank shall be no lower than Assistant Special Agent in Charge) may make an application for an order authorizing a common carrier, public accommodation facility, physical storage facility, or vehicle rental facility to release records in its possession for an investigation to gather foreign intelligence information or an investigation concerning international terrorism which investigation is being conducted by the Federal Bureau of Investigation under such guidelines as the Attorney General approves pursuant to Executive Order No. 12333, or a successor order.

(b) Recipient and contents of application

Each application under this section—

  (1) shall be made to—

    (A) a judge of the court established by section 1803(a) of this title; or

    (B) a United States Magistrate Judge under chapter 43 of Title 28 who is publicly designated by the Chief Justice of the United States to have the power to hear applications and grant orders for the release of records under this section on behalf of a judge of that court; and

  (2) shall specify that—

(A) the records concerned are sought for an investigation described in subsection (a); and

(B) there are specific and articulable facts giving reason to believe that the person to whom the records pertain is a foreign power or an agent of a foreign power.

(c) Ex parte judicial order of approval

(1) Upon application made pursuant to this section, the judge shall enter an ex parte order as requested, or as modified, approving the release of records if the judge finds that the application satisfies the requirements of this section.

(2) An order under this subsection shall not disclose that it is issued for purposes of an investigation described in subsection (a).

(d) Compliance; nondisclosure

(1) Any common carrier, public accommodation facility, physical storage facility, or vehicle rental facility shall comply with an order under subsection (c).

(2) No common carrier, public accommodation facility, physical storage facility, or vehicle rental facility, or officer, employee, or agent thereof, shall disclose to any person (other than those officers, agents, or employees of such common carrier, public accommodation facility, physical storage facility, or vehicle rental facility necessary to fulfill the requirement to disclose information to the Federal Bureau of Investigation under this section) that the Federal Bureau of Investigation has sought or obtained records pursuant to an order under this section.